teamED

Building more effective teams for education, projects, and communities

Mar Cano, Erin O'Reilly & Nick Salmon

Foreword by Dr. Daniel Wilson, Project Zero/Harvard University

Illustrated by Tegan Schaper

Overview

Working alone in the world of education has become so much a part of the air we breathe, that we don't give a second thought to common statements heard in professional learning sessions such as: "When you return to _your_ classroom", "I have organized _my_ classroom to achieve…" or "We should coordinate what happens in _each of our classrooms_." In the world of education, working in teams is nearly nonexistent in training and practice in both highly effective schools found around the world and those that struggle to develop relevant teaching and learning experiences in their communities.

teamED takes readers on an interactive journey from the essential elements of forming a team, being thoughtful about the size and type of teams we create, while sharing strategies for sustaining effective teams. Each chapter includes multiple invitations to reflect upon current practices and desired future practices as educators, project teammates, or community partners.

teamED includes a focus on teams in action, teams and transformation, and ultimately a call to action to grow individually and collectively as teams taking on some of the world's greatest challenges. Although this book focuses on the world of education, we have often adapted the team exercises to team projects, business retreats, and community transformation experiences.

The authors include insights from interviews of young people, educators, and community partners with team experiences on six continents including Suzie Boss, Ela Ben-Ur, Katie Cunningham, Bob Lenz, Samson Nyikuri Nyongesa, Milton Javier Pirazán Rodríguez, Derek Peterson, Rose Poka, Amaris Salazar, Kavita Tanna & Willy Wijnands.

Acknowledgment of Ancestors

We are connected to numerous generations who have made our presence possible. As authors of this book, we acknowledge the Salish, Kootenai, Abenaki, Lenni-Lenape, Basque, and Catalonian ancestors who created the communities in which we now live and work. We are grateful for the continued presence and spirit amongst us.

Foreword

"Collaboration is the essence of life. The wind, bees and flowers work together, to spread the pollen."

— Dr. Amit Ray, Author. Uttarkashi, India

When working in teams becomes the norm, and the flow in our schools and communities, we will truly prepare the next generation of resilient learners for the highly collaborative world beyond the school walls.

Insights from Dr. Daniel Wilson, Harvard University

This book found me at an interesting moment. A few weeks ago, I served on a jury for the first time. Now before you roll your eyes, consider this: it is one of the few civic duties we have in our democracy. In contrast to paying taxes, abiding laws, and voting, it is the only one that requires *teamwork*. That's right. As citizens we are expected to critically collaborate, not just pay what we owe, follow rules, or fill out a ballot. And so, for a week, I attentively took notes alongside thirteen total strangers, each very different from one another. Our ages and skin color ranged. Some dressed formally while others donned flip-flops. One juror became a citizen just this year. The only thing we had in common was our shared responsibility: to weigh the evidence and collectively render a verdict. When the hour for deliberation finally arrived, I confessed that I was nervous: Would we work well together? How would we debate, disagree, and decide? How could *this* be one of our core democratic responsibilities when we have so little direct preparation for collaborating?

Of course, apart from jury duty, working together is something we humans have been doing for quite a long time. The survival of our earliest hunting and gathering clans depended on dividing up roles and sharing responsibilities. Existence hinged on passing lessons, skills and knowledge to the next generation. Some groups did this better than others, and flourished. Others struggled and were unable to learn and adapt. And for thousands of years, our collective knowledge about effective collaboration was divined from evocative allegories and suggestive scriptures. That is, until 1924.

This book arrives exactly one hundred years after Elton Mayo began the first field studies that produced findings on team effectiveness. His research at the Western Electric Hawthorne Works factory was hardly perfect. In fact, he stumbled upon the now infamous Hawthorne Effect -how the awareness of being observed can produce positive impacts on performance. However, it was a starting point in building scientific knowledge about teams. Nestled in his control-group findings was this insight: work performance was often more effective when done in teams. Mayo unknowingly set in motion a century of studies and experimental practices each aimed to better understand the conditions of effective teams such as belonging, trust, and interdependency. From hospital teams to musical groups, sports teams to juries, hundreds of researchers have examined the elusive question of what makes a team work well. Belonging, psychological safety, trust and interdependence are just a few concepts that have emerged over decades of research in countless contexts. And our guides in this book eloquently invite us to considering this question in the context of education.

I've spent over thirty years as a researcher at the Harvard Graduate School of Education's Project Zero exploring why and how we can bolster collaboration in schools. Teaching teams, student projects, and community advisory boards are each opportunities to develop the vital skills we need in a flourishing democracy. Each offers moments to create a shared vision and raise concerns. To enact processes of civil critique and generative dissent. To engage in co-constructing solutions to large and small challenges that we face in our communities. While we hope we do this well, it is difficult work for many teams in schools to do naturally. Doing this well requires us, as educators, to have reflective experiences in teams from which we learn and co-develop best practices. Otherwise, what we, our learners and our communities learn simply perpetuates polarization and individualism. Luckily, we needn't start empty handed. The authors of this book provide us a map to chart a productive path forward.

The tips and tools offered by Cano, O'Reilly, and Salmon are a treasure to those of us who might be nervous about leading and participating in teams. By focusing on the essential conditions, such as trust and purpose, they help us understand how to support others in the initial team moments. They offer strategies for critical processes, such as decision-making and navigating conflict, that can serve any facilitator worried about how well their team will work together. The voices from other experts, examples and resources throughout create a wellspring we can revisit to further our teaming practices.

While the world will continue to change in ways we can't predict, what I can foretell is this: collaboration in teams will continue to play a powerful role in our future. Few problems we face in our complex world can be solved alone. Climate change, poverty, radicalized politics are just a few challenges that we as a species will need to solve, and soon. Each will require courageous collaboration among us all. Whether I find myself on a jury, a teaching team, or a community advisory group, I remind myself that these teams are precious moments of social and civic participation. And this book offers us a timely guide for charting a better future.

Dr. Daniel Gray Wilson
Harvard University
September, 2024

Table of Contents

INTRODUCTION
Our shared global context

"Most great learning happens in groups. Collaboration is the stuff of growth. If we atomize people and separate them and judge them separately we form a kind of disjunction between them and their natural learning environment."
— Sir Ken Robinson, world-renowned education expert (2010)

"A journey of a thousand miles starts beneath one's feet."
— Chinese Proverb (6th Century)

Every point of beginning is informed by our past experiences and connections to the world around us.

This chapter is about the global context for education, projects, community, and our stories/origins within it. Our journey is one of getting started (Chapter 1), forming a team (Chapter 2), being thoughtful about the size and type of teams we create (Chapter 3), sharing strategies for effective teams (Chapter 4), teams, learning, and methodologies (Chapter 5), teams and transformation (Chapter 6), and call to action (Chapter 7). Although this book focuses on the world of education, we have often adapted the team exercises to team projects, business retreats, and community transformation experiences. We look forward to hearing how you have adopted and adapted these practices to your setting.

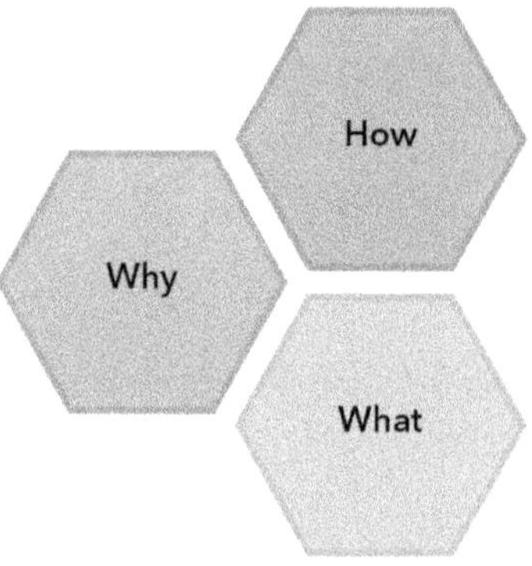

Working alone in the world of education has become so much a part of the air we breathe, that we don't give a second thought to common statements heard in professional learning sessions such as: "When you return to _your_ classroom", "I have organized _my_ classroom to achieve…" or "We should coordinate what happens in _each of our classrooms_." In the world of education, working in teams is nearly nonexistent in training and practice in both highly effective schools found around the world and those that struggle to develop relevant teaching and learning experiences in their communities.

There are some exceptions. The preparation of educators in Finland and other countries requires a master's degree to enter the profession, but ultimately educators may plan together and teach alone. Young educators in Japan work with a master educator for many years, but the focus is on daily reflection, sharing master lessons, and developing successful techniques with other adults, not directly teaching with teams of educators and larger groups of learners.

When educators work alone, learners suffer from the high level of variability in experience and skill between the proverbial Ms. Smith and Mr. Jones, each of whom is working diligently to solve all the problems of the universe on their own in isolated boxes along anonymous corridors.

That isolation leads young educators in the United States to prematurely leave the profession, often after spending fewer years in the profession than they spent preparing to be an educator and long before their student loans are paid off. Allison Zamuda notes that the majority of American educators have one year of experience (down from a majority of 15 in 1987-88) (p. 152). That is a tremendous waste of human capital, a disservice to young learners, and an opportunity to rethink the education, training, and daily life of educators.

The world beyond K-12 education is filled with work opportunities that emphasize collaboration, communication, creativity, and critical thinking; skills needed in a constantly changing world, and somewhat ironically a part of nearly every mission, vision, and value statement of K-12 schools around the world. Simply stated, success in education and in life, requires teamwork.

A breakthrough moment in the development of this book came to Nick after meeting Mar Cano at the second Revolution in Education Congress hosted by Gimnasio Los Caobos in Chia, Colombia. Nick had previously worked with Erin O'Reilly on the Lessons of a Seasoned Furniture Whisperer for the University of Melbourne's Innovative Learning Environments and Teacher Change (ILETC) Transitions 18 conference and proceedings. The combination of sleep deprivation and delayed flights led to the "aha" moment that of course, a book about team collaboration needed to be written by a team. From that moment onward, the book actively incorporated the insights of educators practicing on multiple continents and reflections on the territory our team covered over the course of five years. When it is important, we identify the contributions of individuals by name. Otherwise, these words represent our collective effort to explore, challenge, and inspire each other and each reader to build upon this work.

This book provides tools for educators to create and sustain the cultural conditions for teamwork, build effective teams, make decisions as a team and apply that power to project-based learning, design thinking, flexible scheduling, and much more. The concepts explored within these pages can be applied to any organization and at any level, from young learners to educators and administrators, and in the world of work, nonprofits, and government service.

This book focuses on the value of teamwork in the world of education. We aspire to impact educational experiences at a global scale. Approximately 1.3 billion young people are between the ages of 5-18 around the world. The ratio of educators to learners varies from community to community and from country to country, but nearly 60 million people work in the field of PK-12 education. If we influence the practice of 10% of the educators, those 6 million people will help 130 million young people create a culture of trust, create effective teams, and acquire team decision-making skills that will last a lifetime.

The Why

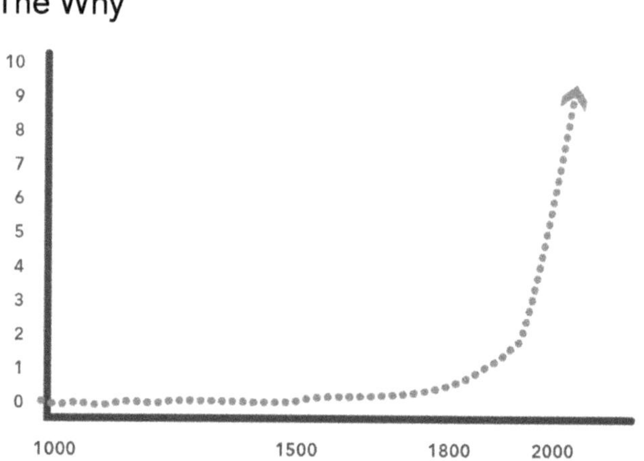

Figure I.1 Increase of Population, Global Temperatures, Technology

The world is changing rapidly. Global population continues to rise, along with a steep ascent in temperature and increased use of technology, energy, and water. These disruptions are linked to civil and economic strife, war, and related conflicts all around the world.

High school graduation rates in the United States remain in the 80% realm with half of those who graduate seeking access to tertiary education in technical colleges, community colleges, and universities. Half of those who initiate higher education complete programs in 4-6 years, often with significant debt accumulated by both graduates and those who do not complete their degree. If you are keeping score, that means that of every 100 learners entering year 9; 80 complete year 12; 40 continue to college, and 20 complete college. The net result is that a significant portion of US citizens experience higher levels of unemployment and lower levels of weekly wages when employed. Another paralyzing concern is the relevance of a university degree in a rapidly changing world.

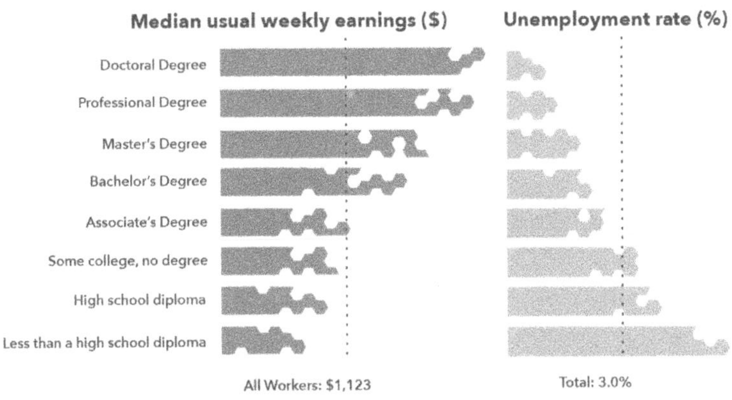

Figure I.2 Earning and unemployment rates by educational attainment, based on US Department of Labor 2022

In *World Class Learners*, Yong Zhao links the rise of social strife to decreased access to economic opportunities fueling a vicious circle of disruption of access to education and lowering future economic opportunities. These settings often lead to the radicalization of groups and destabilization of governments that might otherwise be able to educate the next generation of entrepreneurs needed to tackle climate change, healthcare, and disparity of wealth. Simply put, the world is having a hard time getting along, and having more people educated using 19th (and occasionally 18th) century approaches to teaching and learning is unlikely to prepare current and future generations to solve the wicked problems we have created. As Anthony Lake, Executive Director of UNICEF notes,

> Education is the key to a better life for every child and the foundation of every strong society – but far too many children are still being left behind. To realize all our development goals, we need every child in school and learning. (p. 12)

Around the world, access to quality education is strongly connected to improvements to health and economic vitality. Conversely, a lack of completing secondary school is linked to higher levels of poverty, incarceration, and poor health.

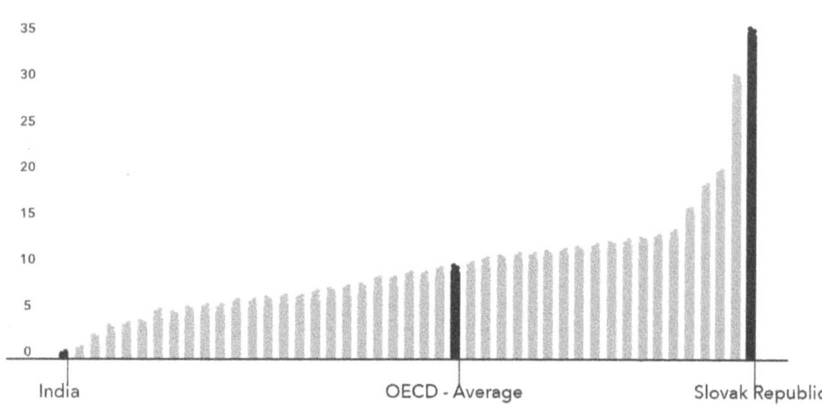

Figure I.3 Unemployment rates by education level

This series of observations may explain much of the conflict in the world, exaggerated by decades-long interventions by wealthy nations in those same areas of conflict. If you are not angry, you are not paying attention. Less-educated people are being taken advantage of across the globe, and access to education may be one of the very few paths available to address each of these conflicts in our environment and social fabric.

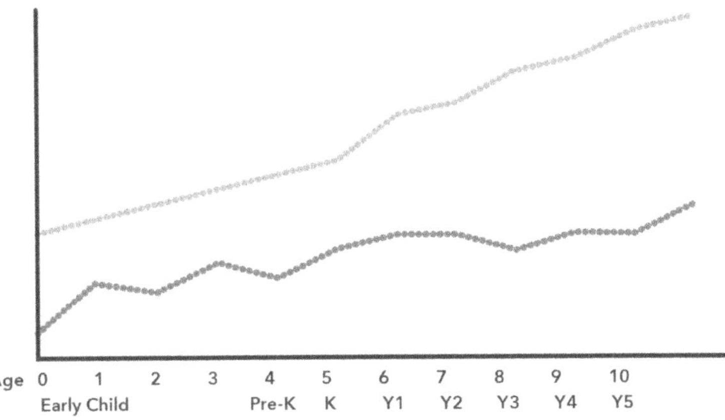

Figure I.4 The Widening Gap

Perhaps the most compelling reason to work as a team is to address the inequity of basic learning experiences that exaggerate the achievement gaps that begin at birth (or before) and extend through the critical primary school years. We have observed numerous examples of parents who understand that some educators are more effective than others, and therefore fiercely advocate for their child to be placed with that educator. Parents who do not understand that there is any difference between educators, who accept the educator their child is assigned to, or do not understand that there is even a game to be played in this realm, experience a widening gap in a few short years. We believe that this is unfair to the growth of each learner and diminishes the potential of every educator.

The How

It is beyond time to think differently about our future. Rather than advance a single idea, we must advance many and choose the best aspects from each. We must become comfortable with failing early and often and, perhaps most importantly, sharing what we learn from each success and failure. Our time is short. Millions around us feel "the fierce urgency of now," do we? The persistence of the global pandemic has provided numerous opportunities to reimagine all aspects of teaching and learning, including how to support working as a team.

The What

This book, this collaboration, advances a few simple propositions. First, we are more creative and resilient when we work as teams, but we need help creating effective teams. Second, we can improve our collective skills when we practice making decisions and improve our commitment to decisions when more people are engaged in the decision-making process. Third, we can discover the joy and wonder of creating evidence of what we know through projects, design thinking, and flexible scheduling, among others.

We hope that each chapter prompts you to ask questions of your own, rethink how you state and prioritize those questions, and ultimately act upon what is most important to you, your team, and your community. It is the essence of the hopeful and revolutionary work we do around the world, and hope it inspires you to do the same.

A few notes about the format of this book
Periodically you will encounter a gray text box where we have included the dialogue between the authors during the development of the book.

*The gray box is also used to share **Other Voices, Practical Experiences,** and a series of **Team Challenge** offerings that we hope you will find helpful during the development of your team.*

You will also see the bee graphic from the book cover prompting you to add your own comments, mind maps, diagrams, drawings, and emerging ideas.

These spaces are meant to be a prompt for those ideas, but please don't feel limited to contributing only when prompted. We hope that by the time you have finished reading this book, it feels more like a personal journal of your own thoughts woven together with what you have read and been prompted to think about. If you are willing to share your journal with the world, please share your insights with us.

Starting from Our Origins

Nick often shares that he is a ninth-generation educator. His namesake was born in France in 1700 and began a string of K-20 educators in various branches of his family. Nick's next ancestor of the same name continued the tradition and wrote or edited sixteen books on education in France and England between 1773 and 1827. Some people grow up in families of bankers, lawyers, doctors, building contractors, and law enforcement professionals. Nick grew up with numerous aunts and uncles who were educators and/or artists. Of the 17 cousins in his mother's generation, 9 were educators and/or artists. When that group is expanded to include spouses, an additional five or six fall in that category. His father had an equally large number of cousins, with a similar distribution of educators and artists. The value of education and being an educator was the air Nick breathed from birth. When Mr. Guthrie gave him his first opportunity to tutor two brothers from Guatemala in the basics of mathematics using his recently acquired elemental Spanish, it was as natural as being asked to show someone how to tie their shoes (although, as a parent, 30 years later he can say that teaching someone to tie their shoes is not as easy as should be).

Nick was a slow learner at nearly every level of education, late to speak, late to read (something not done well until dropping out of college), and challenged in writing, math, and science at nearly every level. The learning challenges before the age of 18 continued in the lectures, seminars, and design studios of his college education where he inevitably grasped the potential of a design studio challenge after he turned in his work, received feedback, and more importantly, saw 20-120 other approaches to the same project developed by classmates.

Those collective experiences represented an odd preparation for becoming an educator, but several people nurtured that potential as they saw him working with his peers or working with younger students on similar design challenges one to five years after he had struggled with a similar exercise. Perhaps if he had spent the equivalent amount of time on his own work, he may have grown more quickly as a designer and student. By that time, he had been breathing the air of education for nearly 25 years, and the transition to graduate school and teaching was the obvious next step for someone who was cautiously embracing adulthood.

When Nick was offered the opportunity to teach in graduate school, he was fortunate to be linked with two seasoned educators who were interested in the perspective he brought to the effort, but not above redirecting his youthful energy in front of the group of 60-75 young designers they shared in common. That experience, combined with his understanding that designing and building buildings was a cooperative experience, informed his passion for teaching as a team, rather than the persistent view in the profession that designers should emulate Ayn Rand's Howard Roark, capable of spontaneously conceiving and executing ideas that sprung fully formed from their brains.

That team of educators was committed to developing the skills of every learner -- sharing dozens of approaches to what is now called design thinking -- rather than assuming every learner arrived with those skills. Education and brain research have since confirmed that none of us are born with artistic, athletic, mathematical, or scientific talent. Outward appearances of "talent" come from thousands of hours of practice including frequent failure and recovery while developing enduring persistence.

Mar, however, is a first-generation educator. Born into a working-class family, all her grandparents –originally from the south and center of Spain– emigrated to the city of Barcelona in search for a better future around the 1950s. Although they were first established in the so-called 'barracks' in the hills of Montjuïc, at the turn of the 1970s they were relocated to the estate houses in the suburbs. Therefore, her parents settled in the outskirts of a nearby town, Badalona. That neighborhood had been created as part of a new housing plan for relocating low-income families, and that turned it into one of the ghetto districts in Barcelona with many Spanish speakers coming from all over Spain.

Moreover, despite her parents graduating only in elementary education, they began to work at the early age of 14 for economic reasons. Starting as apprentices in two different fields, a textile factory and a mechanic garage, they both progressed in their professional careers because of their aptitudes and skills. Her humble family's example and support encouraged her to dream big and focus on her studies to achieve great things in life. Thus, even if she wasn't the most brilliant student in class, her hard work and perseverance together with her abilities led her to succeed in her academic path, always with good grades. However, she affirms that although she never liked studying or all the amount of hours it implied for her; she loved learning from every opportunity in whichever context, and she has proved she still does. In the end, not only was she the first one in her family to go to university and get a degree, but she also managed to get a second one as well as two masters' degrees. Now, she is one of four educators in her whole family.

In any case, finding her passion took her a while and she had to overcome failing first. Although she used to play as a teacher when she was a kid, with her small blackboard and the colorful pieces of chalk, she didn't have a clue what she wanted to become when she had to make one of her first decisive choices ever. In high school she had chosen to follow the scientific branch, so she studied chemistry, physics, math and technical drawing. Besides, she was told she could study anything she wanted, because she had been one of the best students in her promotion. She began a degree in architectural science, yet her unsuccessful efforts caused her to fail many of the courses in the first semester and, even after retaking tests and passing them, she finally decided to quit after one and a half years. Her true search began at that inflection point, taking her time to look for what her real vocation could be. Once she found out about her passions, that same year she took up a degree in Teaching English as a Foreign Language (EFL) in Kindergarten and Elementary School. And since then, she has enjoyed everything she has done in her professional life as an educator.

That 'waha' moment was the changing point that ignited her eagerness to become the best EFL teacher she could ever be. That was the main reason why, after finishing her first degree and starting to work full-time as an EFL teacher, she felt the need to grow her English skills even more and to enhance her professional development. She made the decision to carry out her second degree in English Philology, so that she could teach other age groups and even adults. One year after finishing, she would start her first MA in Construction and Representation of Cultural Identities (specializing in English-speaking countries); and once again, a year later, she would start her second MA in Research and Change in Education. Such a passion for the educational world has moved her to transform education from within the system and to aim at becoming a mindful and reflective educator.

One of the most meaningful changes in her professional career as an educator was when she realized that, though she was meant to teach EFL, first there were other essential issues that needed to be covered for every single student as a premise for any kind of learning: a socioemotional healthy environment. This had a myriad of implications, such as the relationships between teachers and students, types of learning, learning difficulties and talents, the ways of teaching and learning, and much more.

This is when she broadened her mind to deal with other pedagogical concerns related to education and the nature of learning beyond teaching and learning EFL. As a result, apart from taking roles as Head of the Foreign Languages Department, Mar also took up the role as the Pedagogic Coordinator for the whole school from Kindergarten to high school in the same school she had been working for more than a decade. She became a coordinator in an innovation process of a network of 10 schools in Catalonia, and also, she has also been engaged as a teacher trainer, which she currently loves doing worldwide.

Consequently, her experience in the educational field, and in others, has allowed her to go through a wide span of collaborative and teamwork practices in both micro and macro contexts. In that sense, she thinks that teamwork can be trained, enriched and transferred from any other situations in our personal lives. For instance, she recalls her experience as a 4x100m relay runner in high school.

Many people may know the basics in this sort of athletic race. However, you can't tell about its intricacies unless you stop, do some research, and think carefully about them. It implies more than the simple sum of individual efforts and talents. It requires specific skills for each member of the team depending on the position they hold. It requires communication. It requires core values like respect, empathy, and trust: respect for every member's skills, which need to be complementary; empathy to put ourselves in each other's shoes at every single moment during the race, and trust when it comes to giving and receiving the baton without being able to look at each other, and mostly when it comes to believing that every single team member will do their best for the team's benefit. She believes that her team was successful for several years because of, their hours of training, their reflection when failing, and the leadership of their inspirational coach.

Erin's journey in education is one filled with many great influencers from the educational field, beginning with her parents and family. Being born and raised in Missoula, Montana to two loving and supportive school teachers and surrounded by family who taught in K-12 and higher education, she was afforded many opportunities to interact with schools from a multitude of different perspectives. She is the oldest of three girls while also being the middle sibling with an older brother and sister. With lots of nieces and nephews, aunts and uncles, and many cousins, her family is big and beautiful. The larger her family has grown, the stronger the bonds and support. Growing up in such a gorgeous place with such an amazing support network, she thrived in her environment. This sense of belonging, love and support has shaped her as a person and professional, seeking to pass it on in her work as a key distinguisher in her purpose and mission in education. Education was and continues to be a core value, a cornerstone of the person she is today and educator who people not only learn from but value and embrace as part of their educational team guiding them along their own journey.

Like Mar, Erin also experienced that aha moment - when discovering her passion for teaching. This passion ignited the driving force behind her work in education. Starting at a young age of playing school, then coaching travel ball and high school sports after graduating from high school. Her love for teaching was always there but it wasn't until she was able to take her passion for politics and history, and work with high school students to ignite their own curiosities and interests, did the sparks fly.

Teaming and collaboration seem obvious to someone who has been involved in teams her entire life. Her experiences have led her to loudly advocate for the importance of teaming and collaboration to foster essential elements such as empathy, compassion, trust, community, and a sense of belonging. At the foundation of the work shared in this book, you will find her teaming at every level. A collection of experiences that have shaped teammate Erin is in her personal and professional life.

After studying political science and history at the University of Montana and obtaining her Montana Teaching License in Comprehensive Social Studies, she worked as a behavioral intervention specialist. She worked on countless teams, developing strategies and plans for school-wide interventions and supports, and individual students struggling within those systems. She served as an advocate and teammate.

After gaining this invaluable experience, she taught high school social studies. In this position, she was a teacher, department chair, coach, and mentor. She collaborated with students to create opportunities for them to be inquisitive and explore the world around them from a multi-perspective approach. She worked with her students, families, community partners, and colleagues to support each student during transitional periods, specifically from junior and senior year of high school to college or their next step post-secondary schooling. She advocated and created teaming opportunities to collaboratively build mutually beneficial sustainable partnerships that identified solutions and systems that supported students and families. She worked with a variety of partners on a variety of teams to identify strategies, curriculum, and systems that could be used to individualize support for student and collegial growth and development towards their goals.

During this time, this passion grew to a desire to impact not only her students in her classroom but her K-12 colleagues, aspiring educators, educational leaders, and policymakers. She decided to begin working on her Master's in Educational Leadership. She completed her degree and obtained her Montana Administrator License. It was at this time that she was afforded the opportunity to teach courses for the Teaching and Learning Department in their Teacher Education Program at the University of Montana while also working on her Doctor of Education in (at first) Educational Leadership with an emphasis in Higher Education. However, inspired by her work with teacher candidates and drive for change rooted in education and development, changed to a Doctorate of Education in Teaching and Learning.

Erin's work in higher education has allowed her to work through a multi-dimensional approach and see through multiple lenses when viewing the perennial tensions and more recently developed issues in education. While engaging in this work, she serves as an active faculty member serving on committees, conducting research, publishing, presenting, planning conferences, and taking on an active role in her state and national accreditation process. She works with teacher candidates in the classroom and in their clinical experiences. She collaborates with candidates, colleagues, and community partners to support a successful transition from college and their professional program to their career.

These opportunities have led her down a path guided by her vision and purpose for her role in education. She is an advocate for reimagining school. In order to do this, she believes we must reimagine what it means to be a teacher. As educators we fulfill many roles, many we are trained for along with others we are not. We take on these roles because they are necessary to meet the needs of our students. Many times we are not just meeting the needs of our students but also our parents, colleagues, and community. We are teachers, learners, leaders, mentors, role models, counselors, and whatever else is asked of us on any given day. In order for teachers to carry that weight and effectively provide a high-quality education for each individual student they must share the responsibility with their colleagues through teaming, collaboration, and shared leadership. She works to curate opportunities and experiences where others can experience the power of the work done in this way and become empowered to continue the work in meaningful ways for others.

Collaborating together to create shared spaces and experiences for learning. She works with preservice teachers and first-year students, co-creating environments where they can begin to reimagine what teaching and learning looks like. A shared space to engage in inquiry, curiosity, and discovery. Where learners feel safe to try new things, expand their pedagogical and methodological practices, apply their knowledge, skills, and abilities in new settings with different students and build on their success while learning from their failures. Providing them with experiences and skills to grow through the uncomfortable moments. Working to become reflective practitioners who are resilient and possess the ability to persist in the profession in meaningful and beneficial ways.

Her journey in education as an ally and advocate, has led her to this collaborative piece with professionals who she admires and strives to learn from with every opportunity she is afforded. These invaluable partnerships and experiences have provided her with insights and wisdom she continues to cultivate and have continued to fuel her passion and drive to embrace teaming and collaboration as not only a possibility but a necessity that needs to be shared in ways where others embrace it and are empowered by it.

> *Tegan's Impact*
> *After years of researching, writing, interviewing, and collecting potential images, charts, and diagrams for teamED, we reached out to Tegan to create a unified approach to the graphic design and illustration of the book. Her questions sparked new ideas from the entire team and opened new spaces for you to contribute your insights. Every team benefits from the arrival of a new teammate with new insights into the work of the team.*

Your Turn: *What is your story?*

Our Collective Story

During the evolution of this book, a key shift in thinking led to the discovery of our collective voice, rather than three distinct voices. That change began with stripping away elements that were most effective as appendices and launching the discussion of teamwork with a chapter on the essence of every successful and thriving team, on those basic keys a team needs to be based on, like trust and communication. We eventually dropped the appendices but included links in the chapter notes found throughout the book. This collaboration was another of many examples of our YES, AND, BECAUSE approach to developing the book: listening to and validating what each of us offered, expanding upon the potential of those ideas, and taking the work in a new direction.

Therefore, this book begins with trust prior to covering the topics of team formation and team decision-making in order to strengthen the collective experiences of educators, learners, and communities who desire to integrate project-based learning, thinking-based learning, design thinking, flexible timetabling, and much more into their practices. It is common to ask young learners to work in teams or to collaborate with others without developing those skills in advance. The importance of teamwork and collaboration is also promoted by educators who often spend their sadly very short, or occasionally too-long, careers working alone. Young learners are quick to blow the "bs whistle" when they realize that teamwork and collaboration must not be very important if none of the adults around them ever visibly work together.

We are fortunate to work with schools and communities around the world on the transformation of teaching and learning and, as a result, have observed a wide range of practices in more than 10,000 learning environments. We have heard educators offer many explanations to learners who complain about the lack of collaboration and teamwork among adult role models. Educators respond that learners don't see the hours they spend working with their peers in preparation every day. That is true, and that is also the point. Hiding collaboration from learners conceals the insights that emerge from learning from others.

In our work, we have witnessed other common challenges to teamwork. The most vocal learner takes charge of the group and convinces their peers to implement their ideas. This is quickly followed by the statement **"I AM THE ONLY ONE WHO IS _REALLY_ DOING ANY OF THE WORK,"** followed by an exasperated sigh of teenage angst.

We believe that the quality of teaching can be dramatically improved through visible team collaboration, beginning with drawing educators out of their siloed boxes into shared and visible planning centers where they can connect with other educators every day. The next step would be to organize the school day, week and year to intentionally create common planning time with a focus on sharing key insights into the groups of learners that educators support in common. Several steps beyond that include interdisciplinary, team-teaching, and project-based learning within varied blocks of time. But we are getting ahead of ourselves.

We hope that you will quickly incorporate the insights and strategies in this book into your future practices and share what works, what could be better, and what's missing with us soon. Please send us your insights:

teamed.book@gmail.com

So let's get started. What does it take to create a great team? Trust, a common sense of purpose, and great communication. We will take up all three in the next chapter.

CHAPTER 1: GETTING STARTED
Trust, Purpose & Communication

"I can do things you cannot, you can do things I cannot; together we can do great things."
- attributed to Mother Teresa, Nun & Missionary. Calcutta, India

"I learned that I work harder and smarter in a team than alone. I understand the power of adding more smart people to the group when we are not sure of which way to go. I have found unsubstantiated opinions usually to be meaningless BUT that substantive and articulated intuitive gut feelings are worth their weight in gold. I learned that people WANT to be a part of a GOOD team – an effective team; but they neither know how to create nor sustain one. I see that people need to strive for something bigger than themselves, and that material rewards will not fill their deepest longings. I know that tools matter a lot, and the training to use those tools matters MORE than the tools themselves."
- Derek Peterson, Institute for Community and Adolescent Resilience (ICAR-US). Lidgerwood, North Dakota (2021)

"You develop relationships, and through relationships, you trust people more, you can be more vulnerable, you can be honest about the things that are really challenging and hard about that and that you're struggling with, and seek support from those people, particularly when the groups aren't too big. It feels safe that you can say what needs to be said, and that can be discussed in a fair and honest way. It comes down to relationships. The more you work together, the better the relationship, the better the outcomes."
- Louise Whitaker, Primary School Educator, Macquarie College. Wallsend, Australia (2022)

We are often told that there is no "I" in "TEAM", but the critical letter is "T". There is no team without Trust. With trust, we can act on our shared purpose, and with trust, we can be open in our communication.

When working in teams, there are some essential requirements for them to truly succeed. Your experiences with teams probably include successes and challenges. We might gravitate towards or shy away from teaming. We might thrive in some teams and not in others. Experiences with teams are vast and diverse. There is a variety of variables that we might think about when considering teaming. So, what conditions can you think of that set the ground for successful collaborative teamwork? Take your time and identify them here:

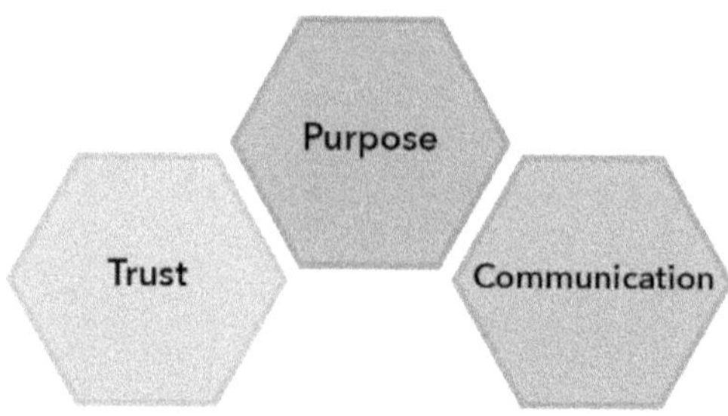

There are consistent elements that present themselves as foundational to effective teams. These elements include **trust**, **common purpose**, **effective communication**, and knowing ourselves and the **biases** we hold. To lay this foundation, we encourage teams to focus on cultivating these elements through the language they use, common agreements and routines they establish, their cultures of thinking, and even their environment.

1.1 Trust

In her book *Teaming*, Amy Edmondson (2012) shares the importance of creating a trusting culture, a place where it is safe to share thoughts and feelings. She noted that "when psychological safety is low, they tend to focus more on achieving their own goals rather than cooperative goals" (p. 129). Highly effective teams operate in the "Learning Zone", where there is a high level of safety (trust) and a high level of accountability (Edmondson, 2012, p. 130).

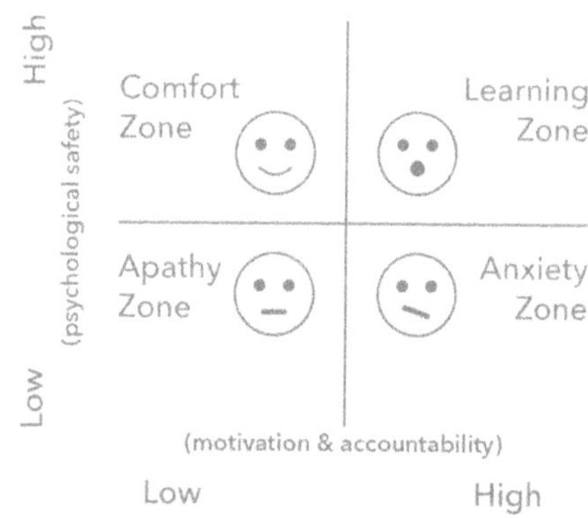

Figure 1.1 Leadership Behaviors for Cultivating Psychological Safety (based on Edmondson).

The need for a team to be operating in the Learning Zone applies to leaderless teams as well. Each teammate contributes to the health of the team through their commitment to maintaining high levels of psychological safety as well as high levels of motivation and accountability. "Psychological safety is a belief that one will not be punished or humiliated for speaking up with ideas, questions, concerns, or mistakes." As Edmondson (2012) notes, "teaming requires awareness, communication, trust, cooperation, and a willingness to reflect" (p. 49).

Inspiring Video

Edmondson, A. (2014, May 4). "Building a psychologically safe workplace". TEDxHGSE.

In our experience, before working with any member of a team, a particular **climate** should be nurtured. Therefore, building an atmosphere of trust, common purpose, and open communication, where every single member of the team can feel safe and welcome, is key.

In our interview with the CEO of PBLWorks, Bob Lenz, he emphasized trust as "the cornerstone of an effective team." He discussed his experiences with teaming and the importance of cultivating high levels of trust. "We practice direct conversations and feedback. We are not afraid to disagree with each other and we always come to some level of consensus, so we share a common message out to the organization we lead". He admits the work is not perfect "but we work through the rough patches. We enjoy each other's company and find time to laugh and share our personal side."

Building **trust** and cohesion can take time, practice, success, failure, restoration, and more practice. However, many teams do not have that much time and need to build trust quickly. We believe that the ideas explored throughout this book can help create trust and cohesion in the time you do have, regardless of what duration that might be. Building trust increases the effectiveness, efficiency, and efficacy of teammates. The exercises in Chapter 4 give teams a sense of having worked together for a lifetime when they might have just begun to work together.

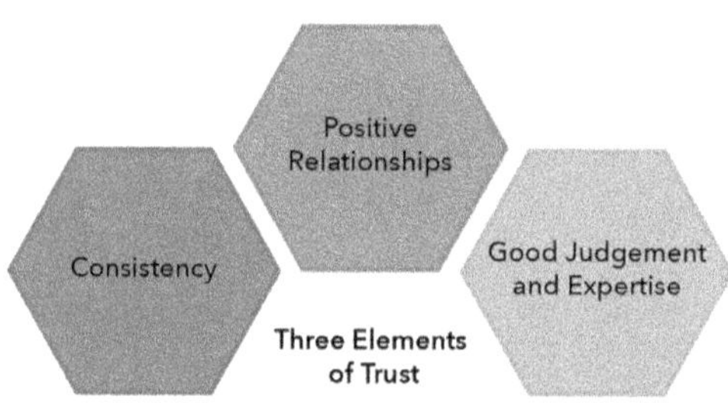

Figure 1.2 Elements of Trust, based on Zenger and Folkman. (2019, February 5)

Zenger and Folkman (2019) expand upon the theme of trust and identify three essential elements, including Positive Relationships, Good Judgement & Expertise, and Consistency. Positive Relationships rely on giving feedback and resolving conflicts as they arise, themes we will return to in Chapter 4. We will continue the discussion of Good Judgement & Expertise in Chapter 2, where we share our expertise with our teammates and learn to trust the ideas, opinions, and co-created contributions as a team. Consistency represents one of the key components of the culture of your team (expanded upon in Chapter 6), your ability to follow through with important details, and to be a role model for your peers who may be working in additional teams of their own.

As we share strategies for cultivating trust within a team, we need to be mindful that there are many strategies to foster trusting relationships, but that trust can be destroyed in the blink of an eye. A word spoken in anger. A confidence broken. A vulnerability exposed. This is why we are sharing ideas and strategies to support you in nurturing a healthy and trustful collaborative environment from the very beginning. We will continue the conversation about trust in Chapter 4 as we discuss positive strategies for team growth. In order to implement these strategies for teaming in meaningful and effective ways and foster environments where teams can thrive, we must focus on laying the foundation for this work.

A foundational pillar for any team is ensuring **psychological safety.** Returning to Edmondson (1999), "team psychological safety involves but goes beyond interpersonal trust; it describes a team climate characterized by interpersonal trust and mutual respect in which people are comfortable being themselves" (p. 354). For that purpose, Barbara Fredrickson found that "positive emotions like trust, curiosity, confidence, and inspiration broaden the mind and help us build psychological, social, and physical resources. We become more open-minded, resilient, motivated, and persistent when we feel safe" (Delizonna, 2017, para. 1). Moreover, the data found in Project Aristotle run by Google showed that this is a critical element to making a team work (Duhill, 2016, para. 35).

The importance of relationship building cannot be overstated when fostering this collaborative environment. The dynamics of a team is developed by the individual members and the relationships formed among members of the team. These relationships can be just as dynamic and complex as the individual members. They depend on many different variables and many times begin before the group even meets. Each individual brings their own **cultural identity** that has been socially constructed and impacts how we perceive the world and those in it. Cultural identity shapes the implicit **biases** or the attitudes, beliefs, and stereotypes that may affect how we unintentionally interact with others.

In order to nurture these safe and trusting relationships within any timeframe, but especially in a short amount of time, it is important to acknowledge the biases we bring with us into spaces of collaboration and the impact these biases have on our relationship with the team and individual members. Teamwork grows from making connections based on both trust and communication, which take into account everyone's biases from the very beginning.

Once every member's individual identity is recognized, it is necessary to create a sense of belonging within the community, where each individual is heard, valued, and empowered. While also sharing common goals and challenges related to accomplishing the shared mission and vision of the team. In this way, connections establish the way each member interacts with each other. In this sense of connectedness, we could think about it in the light of the 'ubuntu' philosophy. As Oviawe (2016) states,

> *ubuntu* is a philosophy of being that locates identity and meaning-making within a collective approach as opposed to an individualistic one. As a result, the individual is not independent of the collective; rather, the relationship between a person and her/his community is reciprocal, interdependent and mutually beneficial. (p. 3)

Even more, along with the social interactions at play, if we want to take any team one step further and deeper, what if those teams were embedded in **cultures of thinking**? According to Ritchhart (2015),

> having a well-articulated purpose lays the foundation for the development of commitment, both to the task and to the learning of the group as a whole. [...] It is this commitment and the recognition of the symbiotic relationship between one's individual learning and that of other group members that help create a sense of community. That feeling of community is further enhanced through a dedication to promoting equity within the group. People often mention shared leadership, valuing everyone's contribution, a nonhierarchical structure, and the leader's being a learner as important actions or characteristics that support the development of equity.

It is not only about sharing common challenges and goals to create a sense of ownership. Before agreeing on some shared goals, it is key to develop shared **norms** to guide the interactions that may take place while working in our teams. Susie Boss & John Larmer (2018) note that;

> the researchers eventually concluded that what distinguished the "good" teams from the dysfunctional groups was how teammates treated one another. The right norms, in other words, could raise a group's collective intelligence, whereas the wrong norms could hobble a team, even if, individually, all the members were exceptionally bright. (p. 83)

As Boss and Larmer (2018) write about Google's Project Aristotle, "The goal of creating shared norms is to promote a classroom culture that values what each person brings while establishing common expectations for the group" (pp. 18-19). "This process shifts the traditional power dynamic and fosters a more democratic classroom" (Boss & Larmer, 2018, p. 18).

Although Boss and Larmer refer to them as 'shared norms', what if this group of statements were labeled as **agreements** instead? Let's stop and consider both words for a moment. If we refer to them as norms, may we assume that an authoritative voice or entity is imposing them from a hierarchical position? On the contrary, if the whole team has a voice and comes to an agreement on what statements will help them all to work collaboratively as a healthy team, the probability that those agreements will be followed increases. In that case, those agreements are the result of the communities' voices as equal participants in the team, and their collective choices, making them co-responsible for their attitudes, behaviors, and actions.

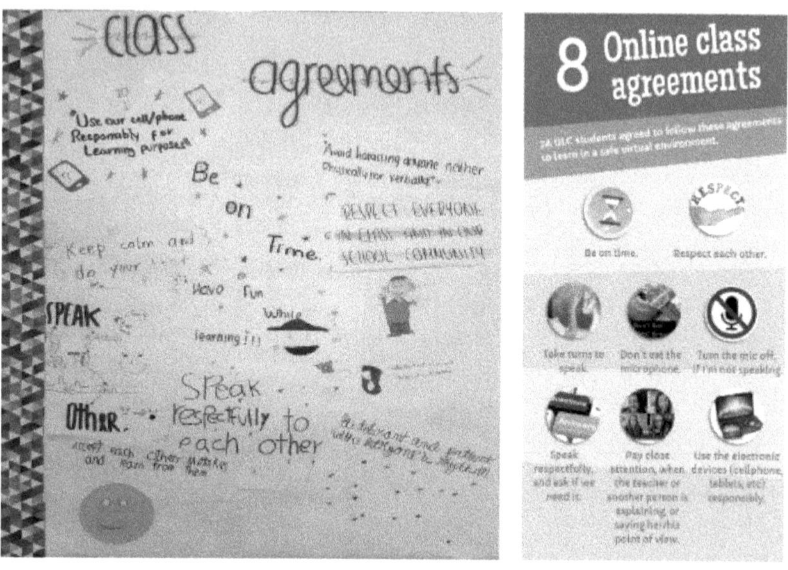

Figure 1.3 (left) Class Agreements 7th grade (Gimnasio Los Caobos, Colombia) 2019/20 School year **Figure 1.4 (right)** Online Class Agreements 7th grade (Gimnasio Los Caobos, Colombia) March 2020 in the emergency Covid-19 pandemic.

> *Our agreements*
>
> *Be present.*
>
> *Be respectful - respect others' opinions and give space when others are speaking.*
>
> *Come with an open mind and be ready to learn and teach.*
>
> *Listen, concentrate, and ask questions.*
>
> *Have a good disposition and a growth mindset.*
>
> *Have fun!*

Figure 1.5 Teachers' agreements in a Reading Workshop about 'Units of Study' with Leca Klam (Gimnasio Los Caobos, Colombia 2019)

With examples like these, we can see how powerful **language** is and how a single word can make a lot of difference. Miguel Ángel Ruiz (1997) was very precise about it in his book *The Four Agreements*. where he stated, 'be impeccable with your words' because "through the word you express your creative power" (p. 34). We will get deeper into language and its power in sections 4.1 and 6.3.

Along with trust, effective communication can be enhanced thanks to non-judgmental and empathetic listening skills based on acknowledging and addressing biases, developing understanding, open and authentic conversations, as well as a mindset of positive and assertive language. Additionally, we can build trust by employing a growth mindset, getting synchronized, and being open to contrary voices. Learning about the other members' origins, cultural identities, values and drivers in life can be helpful to walk a mile in each other's shoes. A teamwork culture that cultivates its members' growth mindset creates the necessary elements for each member to be eager and willing to listen to and to learn from each other. According to Carol Dweck (2006), "the growth mindset is the belief that abilities can be cultivated" (p. 50). Therefore, what if every member of the team shared that belief? How could that contribute to creating a safe team atmosphere that embraces the possibility for all of them to grow and learn something they may not know yet?

Finally, remember how relevant **reflection** may be at this point, in the light of Dewey's (1933) reflective thinking process, of Kolb's (1984) experiential learning model, and Schön's (1983) reflection on the experience. It is not only about tracking, monitoring, and readjusting the relationships created and established among the team members. It is also about reflecting upon them during and after teamwork. They are essential parts of the whole process for fostering positive and successful educational teams and communities.

Regardless of your role in the educational field and the teams you are part of, if you want to initiate change in school culture, focus on improving communication and building trust. Trust can be built through several dynamic exercises. We have included some of our most effective strategies in Chapter 4. We encourage you to use these strategies based on your needs with your teammates and the individuals in your team. Be sure to reflect on the strategies you use and make them visible by noting the exercises that have the biggest impact on your team.

Other Voices:

My best experience working on a team is my current Leadership Team at PBLWorks. There are five of us who share a commitment to the vision and mission of PBLWorks. We have a high level of trust and practice direct conversation and feedback. We are not afraid to disagree with each other and we always come to some level of consensus so we share a common message out to the organization we lead. Of course, it is not perfect but we work through the rough patches. Finally, it is fun – we enjoy each other's company and find time to laugh and share our personal side.

– Bob Lenz (Interviewed by teamED authors on 2020 Jan.)

The exercise below is one of our favorites, inspired by the work of Dr. Josh Garcia, Superintendent of Tacoma Public Schools. We find that these questions release powerful stories that connect people to each other. We hope that you have the same experience with your team.

Team Challenge:

Share your most powerful learning experience.

Many of these experiences come from the distant past, and when they are shared in a new group, they are brought into the present and help to identify what events shaped who we are today. Relationships gain 5, 10, 20 years of connection when those stories are shared. The exercise includes:

> *Think about your most powerful learning experience. EVER.*
> *Give it a name (The day I learned to ride a bike, cooking with gramma, etc)*
> *Who were you with?*
> *Where did it take place?*
> *How did it make you feel? (Mad, Sad, Glad, Scared...)*
> *Why does it remain memorable today?*
> *What would school look like if all learning were that memorable?*
> *Did your experience include examples of failing, recovering, and persisting?*

1.2 Purpose, Passion & Ikigai

Clarify your Core Purpose. What is your core purpose as an educator? And what is your core as part of a team? To know learners well? Content mastery? To develop critical thinking skills? To promote lifelong skills?

Your core purpose may not be clearly stated or broadly accepted in hierarchical organizations, including many schools. Take a moment to identify your core purpose; your ikigai, or reason for being; and return to this question after you have read Chapter 2 Team Formation, and Chapter 4 Teamwork Strategies to add any new insights you may have.

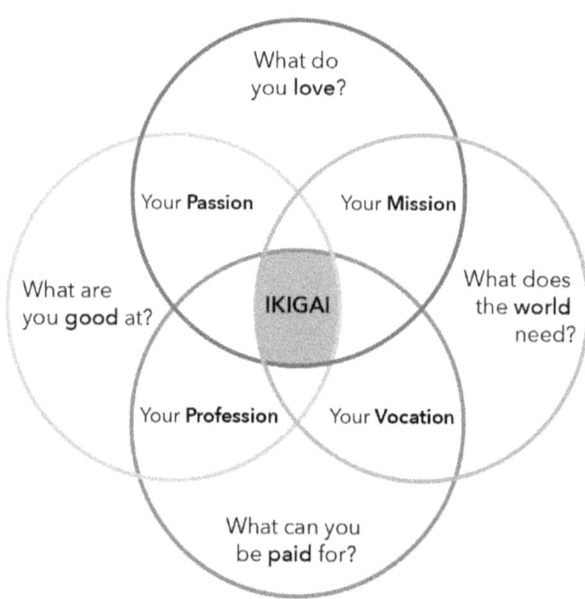

Figure 1.6 Ikigai

Other Voices:

The bus actually got stuck three times during our journey. So the first time it's more like- "This is a challenge we can beat." We all got out and we were all psyched up- "Let's try, let's do this." And then the second time we got stuck, some people started moving away a little bit and were tired. Now the third time it's already dark and the bus is stuck. And this time it's not stuck because of the road. It is because of vegetation on the side of the road, and the bus cannot pass. So we need to work together to make sure the bus goes beyond this point.

– Rose Poka- Emerging Leader Representative-Duke of Edinburgh International Award-Africa, Nakuru, Kenya (2022)

1.3 Your Passion

Share your passions. What are the sources of your passions? What would get you off the bus for a third time? Who does it connect you to? How do you act on that passion each day? How might that common interest help you to create a team with a shared purpose and passion?

Your Turn: What are you passionate about?

Team Challenge:
Making your Values, Vision & Mission visible every day

Identify a recorder for your group and note key issues on a large sheet of paper. Review the Vision, Mission & Goal statements below and provide examples of how they are integrated into learning experiences and daily practice.

GROUP 1
A. **Values- Relationships, Relevance & Rigor**
- Create & support relationships between learners
- Create & support relationships between educators
- Create & support relationships between community partners

GROUP 2
B. **Vision Statement:** Creating a Culture of Learning for All
C. **Mission Statement:** We prepare all students for college/career and success in life by focusing on high student achievement, a "students first" philosophy, and a "whole child" approach to education.

GROUP 3
D. What would learners tell us about their experience of our Values, Vision & Mission statements?
E. What would community partners tell us about their experience of our Values, Vision & Mission statements?
F. What did we learn from the COVID-19 pandemic about our Values, Vision & Mission statements?

Identify a spokesperson for your group and share the highlights of your discussion with the whole group.

Identify Guiding Principles, *for example, "Learners and educators create evidence of our mission, vision, and values every day. Our mission, vision, and values are known throughout the community and could be explained at the check-out line in the grocery store.*

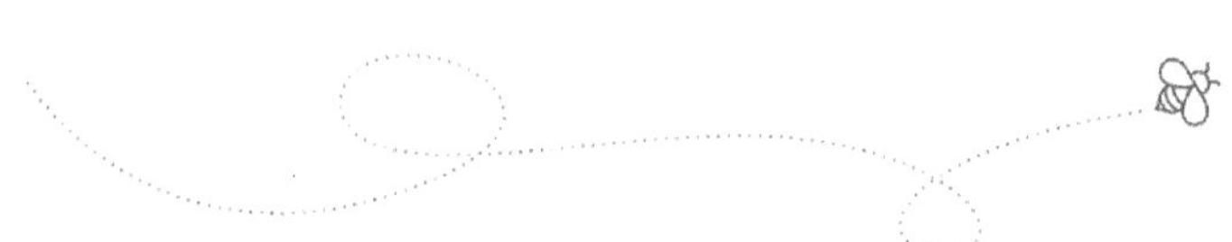

You are on your way to getting started with higher levels of trust (more to come in Chapter 4) and acting with clarity of purpose. Perhaps you are able to readily state your ikigai. That foundation is important before you take on your next challenge, forming your team.

CHAPTER 2: TEAM FORMATION

Accelerating Awareness, Building Credibility, Developing Insight & Sharing Wisdom

"The most powerful form of learning, the most sophisticated form of staff development, comes not from listening to the good works of others but from sharing what we know with others.... By reflecting on what we do, by giving it coherence, and by sharing and articulating our craft knowledge, we make meaning, we learn."

– Roland Barth, Improving Schools from Within (1990)

"Developing relationships is something that needs constant work, from my experience, and getting to know each other in the different ways our personalities play in our role and our job, the different ways we approach problems and challenges. So we all have strengths to offer that group. And as you get to know people, you can really draw on each other's strengths and differences to get the best outcomes. I think it's a byproduct of spending time with people, you get to know each other. You get to know each other's strengths, and where they can really contribute."

– Louise Whitaker, Primary School Educator, Macquarie College. Wallsend, Australia (2022)

Forming a great team requires intention and attention. Teams can be randomly assigned or purposefully formed, but each requires identifying the purpose of the team, the strengths of each teammate, and attention to the growth of the team even when challenges emerge.

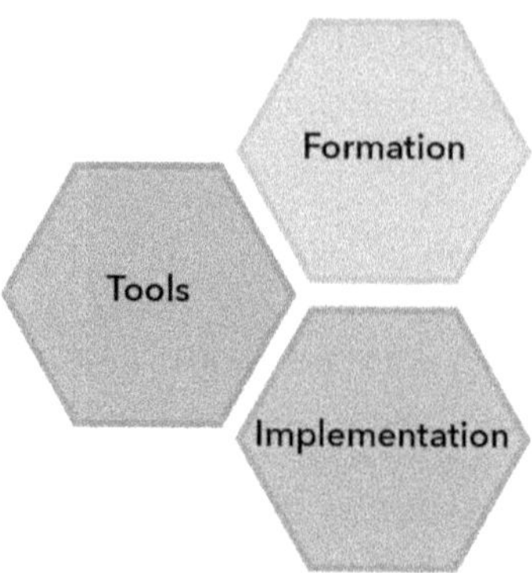

Team composition begins with understanding the strengths of each teammate. We created the simple four-quadrant framework outlined in this chapter to support the creation of great teams. Our teamwork interviews reinforced the notion that great teams are formed when each teammate offers their greatest strengths while developing their greatest needs with support from the team.

> *Other Voices:*
>
> "It was powerful because we truly were all so different that it enriched our abilities to not only learn from one another, but also to learn acceptance, compromise and how to listen openly and willingly."
>
> *- Amaris Salazar, Avante Global School.*
> *Cartagena, Colombia (2021)*

Lisa Kerscher of Brightways Learning noted that a team is not 4 people doing the same thing, but rather "we understand how we complement each other well because no one person can do everything." Ela Ben-Ur, creator of the Innovator's Compass, shared "my favorite projects and team experiences were when I could kind of put that [level of experience] aside and realize that everybody is (an) expert at whatever level they're at."

Philip Hayes (2011) notes that "Each team, even if engineered to an organisational blueprint and designed to represent the prevailing culture, will be unique, often bafflingly so, in its complex human interactions and dynamics" (p. xi). School leaders in Queensland, Australia, shared observations about the composition of teams of traditional and progressive educators. In their experience, when a traditional educator is paired with a progressive educator, the team reverts to traditional practices. When a traditional educator is placed on a team with three progressive educators, they feel isolated and less likely to consider progressive practices. The "Goldilocks" zone is consistently found when one traditional educator and two progressive educators work together in a team.

Jennifer Klein, CEO of Principled Learning Strategies, shared an interesting technique for learners who typically choose their friends as teammates. When teams of friends are first formed, they are asked to appoint a president, vice president, secretary, and treasurer. After those choices have been made, four new teams are formed, one composed of presidents, another of vice presidents, etc. This approach quickly reorganizes the composition of teams and creates opportunities to identify the values that bring each group together.

Other Voices:

"Es que el impacto, creo que con todos los miembros del equipo con que hemos conversado ha sido en lo personal y en lo colectivo. Si bien la mayoría "era un llanero solitario en su centro educativo" y por ende utilizaba la tecnología de forma frecuente, lo que alcanzamos acá fue un nivel superior, acceder a nuevos códigos y fraternidades, que te entregan una autoconfianza, en lo que vienes haciendo, pues ya no estás más solo y puedes estirar la mano y solicitar ayuda, aunque en tu centro puedas ser una isla, hoy esa isla es un nodo dentro de otro red, que es mucho más grande, y eso sí o sí se proyecta en tu contexto más cercano"

"It is that the impact, I think, with all the other team members with whom we have talked has been on both the personal and the collective. Even if the majority "was a free spirit/lone ranger in their own educational institutions" and, consequently, used tech frequently. What we achieved here was a superior level, to access new codes and fraternity, which give you self-confidence, in what you have been doing, as you're not alone anymore and you can stretch your hand and ask for help, although you can be an island in your school, today that island is a node within another network, which is bigger, and that is projected in your closest context."

- Antonio Grezan, representing the founders team of Competencia Digital Cero, Latin America & Spain (2022)

2.1 Formation

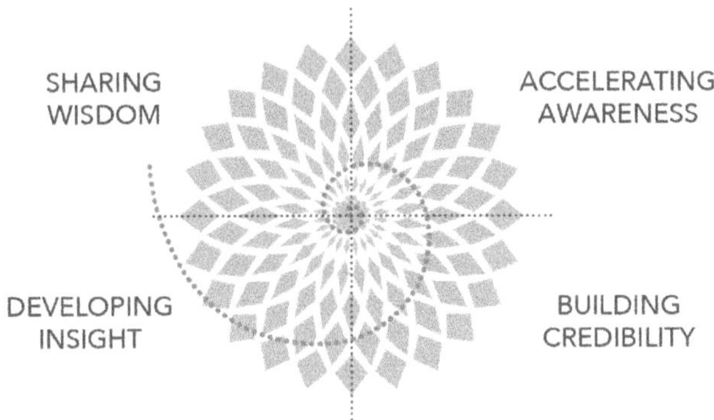

Now let's consider team formation.

More than 20 years ago Nick was asked to teach a professional practice class that had been taught by the same faculty member for the prior 15-20 years. The syllabus he received provided a good framework for the 15-week class which of course was to be taught alone. He quickly recruited a half dozen collaborators who brought the added benefits of additional voices and local relevance to the work. The ponderous 15-week length was broken into a collection of 1-2 week exercises to allow for many opportunities to fail, recover, and persist, rather than building the sum of all knowledge toward one or two high-stakes exams.

On the final day of the class, Nick finally had the needed perspective to realize how the class could have been structured (once again, so similar to his experiences 40 years ago as a young design student). Nick never taught the class again, but on that day, the idea for this book first began to develop, and in the intervening years has been shared with teams of designers, community leaders, educators, and administrators. These ideas apply to careers and projects and, as a result, apply to people of any age, in and out of the world of education and design.

To begin, think of your career or the development of any project as a circle. Better yet, think of it as an ever-growing spiral where each project, each term, or each year represents opportunities for growth.

The first quarter of the circle represents **Accelerating Awareness**; the second, **Building Credibility**; the third, **Developing Insight**; and the final quarter, **Sharing Wisdom**.

Accelerating Awareness

This phase represents the combination of one's formal education and the on-the-job training that follows. The first days in either setting may feel like drinking from a fire hose, and not a position that anyone desires to linger in for long. But there is often much to learn as the world changes around us, so even the most seasoned educator may find themselves frequently in Accelerating Awareness mode. The global pandemic immersed educators in this realm, with a renewed commitment to being a lifelong, life-wide, and life-deep learner. Remember that, in the end, we are modeling what the learners may mostly pick up, our actions, much more than our words.

Learners may find themselves in a similar position. Each new project may be initiated with a phase of Accelerating Awareness - conquering the basic understanding needed to proceed with the project - communication skills, video technology, an understanding of physics, etc.

Building Credibility

There might be a day in every project or career when you have been identified by your peers as the "go-to" problem solver for some aspect of the challenge you are working on. It may be the skills you have developed in technology, communicating with the team or some other realm in which you shine. Perhaps you have been working on one of the critical details of the project that helps the rest of the team to see the whole picture in a new way. This is the moment when you tip from Accelerating Awareness to Building Credibility. The feeling of having achieved Building Credibility cannot be matched, you have arrived! You feel the relief of no longer drinking from that fire hose, that is, managing the overwhelming flow of information that we often encounter early in a project or career, and acknowledgment that you have something of value to share with the rest of the team.

You may not wish to remain here forever, and thankfully Developing Insight lies ahead. Luckily, each member of the team will have something of value to share and you will complement each other. Empowering every single person will be key for a healthy and successful team to perform at its best. Make sure you all find the value or talent in each of you.

What is the difference between Building Credibility and Sharing Wisdom? Think of Building Credibility as the "quick fix" and Sharing Wisdom as the ability to see the whole picture.

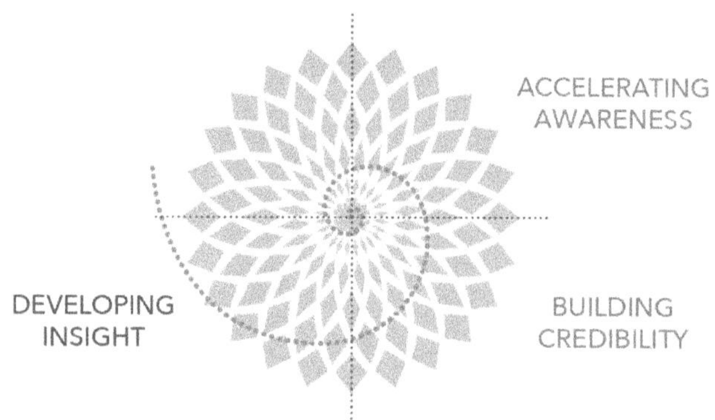

Developing Insight

In some ways Developing Insight is the most difficult role to find yourself in. It requires the ability to slow the learning process down enough to reflect upon and develop each of these insights. They may come from many failures, or a desire to avoid failing once again. It may be that you observe others repeating something that previously challenged you, and that observation leads to your insight. Something once considered routine no longer works for the team, and your ability to develop insight makes the difference between being unprepared for change and thriving in a changing world. A constantly changing world of work moving at a frenetic pace adds to the challenge of Developing Insight. It may be that your ability to observe the world in slow motion and capture those insights is the most important contribution you are making to the team.

Although it is possible to remain in the "Building Credibility" phase of a career and to focus on being the best "go-to" team member, we have found that it can be an exhausting role with an intensity level that might be difficult to sustain.

The person who is developing insight has opportunities to say: "If I had to do it all over I would..." "The next time I would..." We have all had "ah ha" moments after struggling with an issue when we suddenly see our work or the project differently and a better solution emerges. This phase of a career cannot be achieved by accident; it requires a conscious effort to look critically at each decision made, and to assess the impact of those decisions on the project as a whole. Moreover, these insights grow not only from the years of experience, but also from the reflection on that experience (Dewey, 1933); even more, the reflection-in-action and reflection-on-action (Schön, 1983); and also, from going through an experiential learning cycle (Kolb, 1994).

As we move through the "developing insight" phase of a career, these moments occur more frequently and prepare us for opportunities to share our wisdom.

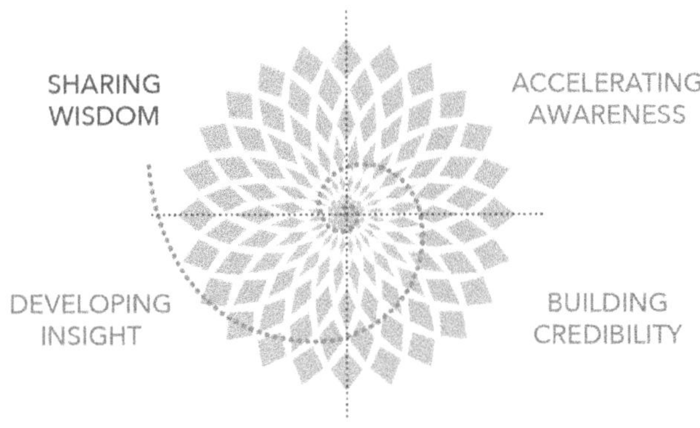

Sharing Wisdom

It is not enough to frequently develop insights and then share them with yourself—"Look how clever I am!" or "I hope I don't do that again." If you are contributing to a team, and you have wisdom to share, time should be made for wisdom sharing to happen frequently. In an educational setting, common planning time may create the occasion to share challenges and insights with each other. It is also helpful to have teammates at other stages in their careers who would benefit from your wisdom.

Even more, sharing your wisdom with others, both from your same field or from very contrasting ones, can reshape, transform, and enrich that wisdom thanks to the connections we can make with someone else's shared wisdom. Let's call it **distributed collective wisdom**. Therefore, everyone who gets involved in that sharing may benefit from it. Moreover, as Peter Senge stated, "Groups dedicated to developing collective wisdom can have dramatically greater effectiveness in what they achieve" (Briskin, Erickson, 2009: p.viii).

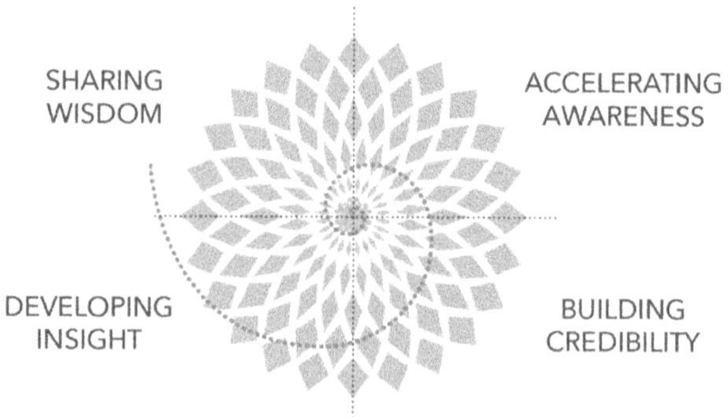

So that's the often-repeated cycle of a career or frequently-repeated cycle of a project captured in four simple steps. Ideally, a highly effective team would include each of these perspectives, rather than each person taking months or years to cycle through each phase.

Our Writing Process

What's next? Let's explore how the teamED tool can shape highly effective teams from our own experience. As an example, here is the narrative that grew out of that experience as we used this tool early in the development of this book.

That day we had a great conversation about what skills we needed as a team for our purpose, the development of this book. We began with a list based on skills some teams of educators often identify as critical to their success:

> *Social and Emotional Learning (SEL)*
> *Time Management*
> *Technology*
> *Project Based Learning*
> *Content Mastery*
> *Lesson Planning*
> *Community Engagement*
> *Other*

However, this list did not exactly fit our purpose of writing a book collaboratively, and we made the decision to modify it to include the skills that the three of us agreed were necessary to co-write the book:

> *Listening Skills*
> *Writing Skills*
> *Big Picture Thinking*
> *Time Management*
> *Technology*
> *Professional Contacts*
> *Community Engagement*
> *Research*

We realized that it was important to define what these items included, what they meant to each of us and to get to a consensus on their meaning, and why they were on the list of skills. Some skills included subcategories, such as communication skills (Listening, Speaking, Writing), which required separating Writing from Listening and Speaking, since we may tend to average our self-assessment across several skills. For example, Nick is more confident in Speaking than Writing; Erin is more skilled in Research; and Mar is more confident in Digital Skills. In addition, our experiences in Research and Critical Thinking vary enough to justify separate categories.

> Listening & Speaking Communication Skills
> Writing Skills (express ideas, edits, comments)
> Big Picture Thinking (Thinking big and acting on details)
> Time Management (managing our time together and apart)
> Digital Skills (writing and publishing platforms, social media, video, etc)
> Professional Networks (education peers, critical friends, industry connections)
> Research (seeking relevant and reliable sources)
> Collaboration Skills (ability to bring best to effort)
> Creativity (Yes, and thinking, openness, ability to express ideas)
> Critical Thinking (ability to assess sources, ideas)

We also aspired to keep the list to ten or fewer items, recognizing that the list could have many more, but would become difficult to complete, or would imply a nuance that doesn't exist. This is also a way to prioritize and focus on the really necessary skills for the shared purpose of the team.

During our next call we determined that the list of skills could be grouped into three big areas, social-emotional wellbeing, thinking and technical:

SOCIAL-EMOTIONAL WELL BEING
> Listening & Speaking Communication Skills
> Collaboration Skills (ability to bring best to effort)
> Professional Networks (education peers, critical friends, industry connections)

THINKING
> Big Picture Thinking (Thinking big and acting on details)
> Creativity (Yes, and thinking, openness, ability to express ideas)
> Critical Thinking (ability to assess sources, ideas)

TECHNICAL
> Writing Skills (express ideas, edits, comments)
> Time Management (managing our time together and apart)
> Digital Skills (writing and publishing platforms, social media, video, etc)
> Research (seeking relevant and reliable sources)

2.2 Tools: Moving Between Quadrants

Not all young peers are Accelerating Awareness and not all seasoned professionals have wisdom to share. For the moment, let's linger in the world of education. As we noted above, an educator is asked to develop many skills to succeed, including Social Emotional Learning, Time Management, Technology Integration, Community Engagement, Global Competency, Content Mastery, Active Learning Methodologies (Project Based Learning, Design Thinking, Inquiry-Based Learning, etc), Assessment and more.

It is common to assume that young educators arrive in the profession with a high level of technical experience but lack the teaching experience to master time management or classroom management skills. Similarly, we might assume that a seasoned educator has conquered time management but continues to be flummoxed by technology. The reality is that the full range of experience is likely to be found on any team, independently of any educator's years of experience. Just as we should not assume that every seasoned educator has wisdom to share in every realm, we should not assume that new educators are entirely in Accelerating Awareness mode. No matter where each team member may find themselves, the potential for growth through practice, reflection, feedback, and revised practice allows for significant shifts. And finding every member's wisdom should be a must.

As you examine the composition of your team, a simple matrix can be developed to allow each person to identify where they would place themselves. In practice, we have found it helpful to first have everyone identify what their team needs to succeed, then lead them through the 4 quadrant explanation, and finally, share the matrix for their individual and collective use.

	AA	BC	DI	SW
Social Emotional Learning				
Time Management				
Technology				
Project Based Learning				
Content Mastery				
Lesson Planning				
Community Engagement				
Other				

When applying this thinking to a project team, the assessment is similar:
- Verbal Communication
- Research
- Technology
- Writing
- Directing
- Video Production
- Making food, art, music, stories, science, etc.
- Etc.

2.3 Implementation: Using the Assessment Tools

As a team, first, develop the list of qualities needed to be an effective team member. Expand upon the list above; but keep it to less than ten items whenever possible. A shorter list allows the team to focus on the essential elements of their work, rather than becoming lost in the details of daily practice. In our experience, assessing a short, memorable set of skills increases the likelihood that the team will use this instrument and process as often as possible.

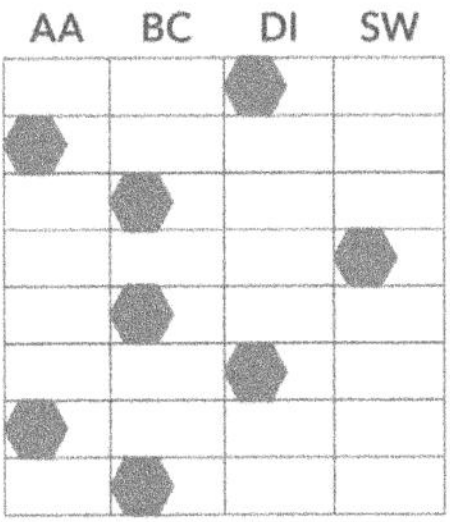

Conduct a self-assessment and share it with your team. If your team members know you well, it could be that they have a different perspective on some aspects, which may make you reconsider your self-assessment. For example, you may not feel your community engagement skills are adequately developed, but your teammates remind you of the many ways you connect to community partners throughout a typical year. Discuss your self-assessment with your peers and ask for feedback before you complete your assessment. Also, look for gaps in your experience and identify areas for potential growth.

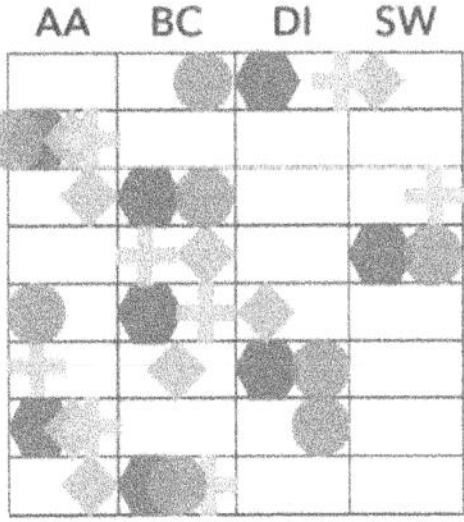

If you are all Sharing Wisdom rock stars, reach out to your administrator and suggest redistributing team members so your skills and experience can be shared with other teams. If your team has a high level of autonomy, you may be able to reorganize yourselves to best meet the needs of the learners, educators, and community partners you work with. The same would be true of teams who discover everyone is Accelerating Awareness.

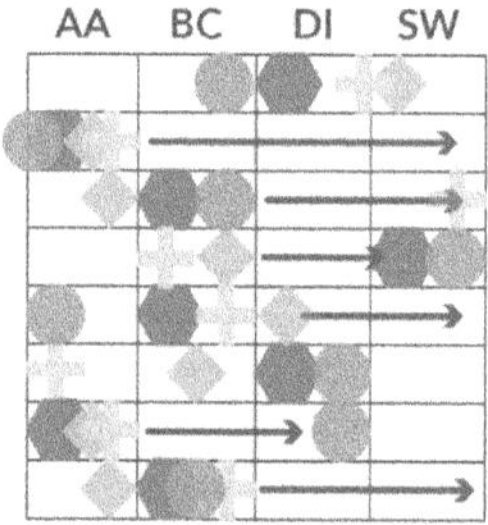

Neither of those two scenarios is likely to occur, but your team may need help in the form of personalized professional learning experiences that allow each person to learn at their own pace and at the pace of the team. Ideally, the team would meet and plan daily and have many opportunities to teach together, provide real-time feedback to each other, and devote time for reflection on current practice. In our experience, working as a well-balanced team nurtures and accelerates the professional growth of individuals and the entire team at rates not previously experienced. Working as a team is a rich learning process with many opportunities to grow and reflect on the journey along the way.

In any possible scenario, there are opportunities to customize your individual and team professional learning experiences. According to Richard Elmore's modes of learning framework (2008), administrators in hierarchical types of organizations could use this tool to frequently monitor the health of a team and to prepare to re-balance teams as team members retire, take leave, are promoted, or are reorganized in other teams according to the needs of the organization. In distributed collective modes of organizations, the team could learn how to self-regulate themselves. Each change is an opportunity to ask themselves "what does this particular team need at this particular moment?", "What do we, as a team, need under these specific conditions?"

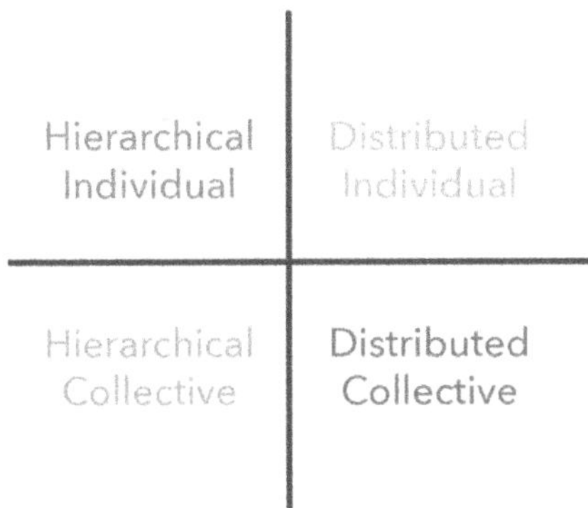

Figure 2.1 Based on the Modes of Learning by Richard Elmore

Teammates may choose to complement this work with different types of personality tests according to the approaches they want to put focus on, such as Strengthfinder, 5 Love Languages, VIA Character Strengths, Meyers Briggs and FourSight, Standout 2.0, Multiple Intelligences, OCEAN, etc. If you want to learn more about and get deeper into your inner traits, you are invited to have a closer look at them all in the chapter notes, and try them!

Nowadays, AI can also be an ally to help us create balanced and diverse teams. For example, EDUTEAMS is an AI software, which was created by the Artificial Intelligence Research Institute and the Spanish National Research Council (CSIC) in 2018, to build teams of learners with a diversity of genres, personalities, and intelligences for more efficient collaboration. We can also use AI to address gaps in our individual and collective experience.

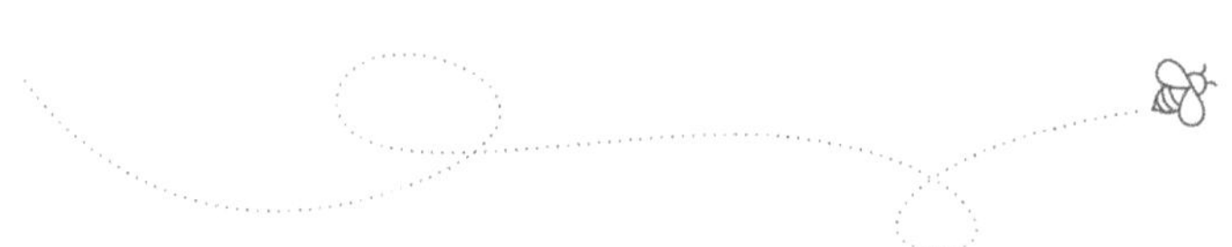

You have identified the skills your team needs to be successful as a group of educators, for a project, or as a community. Agreeing to that group of skills probably required trust, identifying your shared purpose, and listening to each other as you completed your self-assessment and group assessment and discovered your strengths as a team. It is unlikely that anyone noted they had wisdom to share in every category. Perhaps your peers encouraged you to shift your assessment from Building Credibility to Developing Insight. You now have a framework to apply to the territory ahead: the sizes and types of teams.

CHAPTER 3: TEAM COMPOSITION
Team Sizes and Team Types Matter…a lot.

"Individually, we are one drop. Together, we are an ocean."
– Ryunosuke Satoro. Fictional Japanese Character

The size of a highly effective team is intentional. There might be a magic number for effective teams to succeed. As Erickson and Gratton (2007) noted, "Even the largest and most complex teams can work together effectively if the right conditions are in place" (p.3). However, is there a consensus on its ideal size? Likewise, there might be a conclusive recipe for a successful team type. If so, what is it?

For us, not too many and not too few teammates are essential to the success of a team. We concluded that it was more important to have team members who are willing to use a toolbox of strategies and techniques than any specific number of team members. Additionally, successful teams keep in mind their particular context, their formation, and their composition. Moreover, we dare to say that putting a group of people together does not necessarily imply that a TEAM has been created. Every single member of a team can become empowered with a variety of strategies no matter how the team was formed.

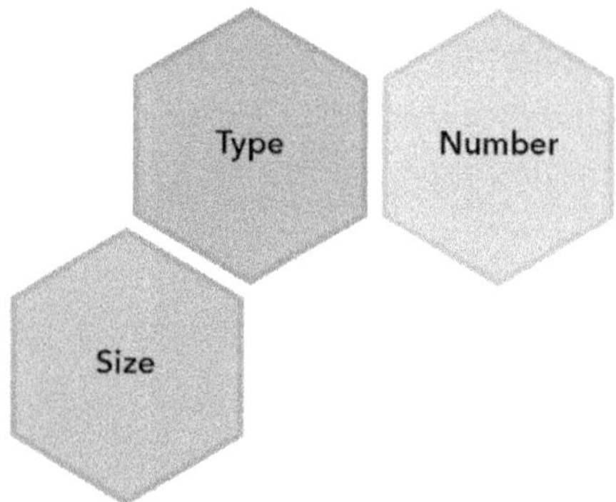

3.1 Team Sizes

Once we know how to assess and balance teams in relation to their strengths, how about considering team size?

Even as one, you can plant a seed and make some change… Imagine if you pair with someone else and let the team grow… Think about how various plants grow together- for example, corn, squash, and beans grow symbiotically.

We have seen a wide variety of team sizes throughout the world of education. For example, EL Education schools across the United States operate under a daily "crew" experience of small groups of learners focused on wellbeing, academic support, and team dynamics. Those small groups are often broken into even smaller groups of three for reflective listening experiences or aggregated into large groups to build school-wide culture. Interestingly, the powerful experiences of "crew" helped to sustain relationships during the pandemic, where each learner had well-established relationships with peers and educators that carried into online learning environments.

Human behavioral science reinforces what we have observed, and many educators have confirmed that groups of three to five are more effective than groups smaller or larger than that range. That is an optimal number, as confirmed by the *Centre for Teaching and Learning* at Western University in Ontario, Canada. Besides, in the context of cooperative learning, small teams may vary slightly to four or five members who become positively interdependent (Kagan, 1985). However, as Avdiaj (2017) points out, several authors have considered that:

> the best team should consist of two people in order to avoid **social-loafing** (Fried, 1991) and **motivation loss** (Kameda, et al., 1992). While others are more general in evaluating the size by considering that it should be small, but large enough to deal with all assigned tasks (Gladstein, 1984; O'Reilly & Roberts, 1977). (p.22)

Moreover, after having interviewed 25 people with experience working in teams on 6 continents, the data analyzed expressed that the size of the teams in the most memorable teamwork experiences they could recall varied from two to even twenty members! This made us wonder, are we talking about 'teams', in their pure essence, or about 'groups' engaged in teamwork? Could then size be an attribute to consider for successful effective teams?

In any case, let's have a look at different team sizes, their potential, and their challenges. The success of a team may not depend on the size, but could definitely contribute to it.

Teams of one

If you are currently a team of one, why not become the team leader yourself and a builder of your own team? And how might you prepare yourself to contribute to an emerging team? Even more, why not get prepared to be an effective team member who can successfully be part of any type of team that aims at fostering a shared and distributed leadership model?

Let us share **an example** of an educator who made a big difference in their learning environments. We are sure you may come up with some more names in your own contexts, or that **you** could even be one of these as well.

Many films and documentaries highlight the image of a lone educator doing transformational work, while limited by the inability to grow another generation of young educators or inspire contemporaries to take similar risks.

Have you ever seen the 2007 film 'Freedom Writers'?

Figure 3.1 Erin Gruwell & Freedom Writers

This was Erin Gruwell's real story put together in a film. She embodied the powerful spirit of a true teacher as she succeeded in transforming her students' lives by fostering an educational philosophy that values and promotes diversity through the power of telling stories.

As a teacher at Woodrow Wilson High School in Long Beach, California, she "encouraged her students to re-think rigid beliefs about themselves and others, reconsider their own daily decisions, and ultimately, re-chart their future" (Freedom Writers Foundation, 2020, para. 8). Later, she became an author, and the founder of the *Freedom Writers Foundation*, where she currently teaches educators around the world how to implement her innovative lesson plans into their classrooms.

Inspiring Stories

Learn more about Erin Gruwell's story and the Freedom Writers Foundation.

Being the best member of your one-person team is your first step, and maybe the easiest one, but don't stop there. Rather than becoming a long-term isolated educator in your silo; focus on playing a new role in another bigger team. Your growing team allows you to impact a wider audience but will require interacting wisely with other team members.

Pairs

The benefits of successful teacher pairs and true collaboration can definitely have a positive impact on the learners, as Cook and Friend (1993) state:

> Collaboration has a direct impact on students, too. For one thing, they receive the benefits of instruction planned by two teachers. It is quite likely that the combined efforts of the teachers are more powerful than any plans that could have been developed by a single teacher. In addition, teachers are modeling collaborative behavior for students, whether it is through co-teaching in the classroom or by participating as members of a school team. (pp. 433-434)

This is where 'co-teaching' is at play. Cook and Friend (2016) identified not a single model, but six models of co-teaching, as the most common approaches that may be applied in different situations taking into account their pros and cons. The six models as defined by Cassel (2019) include:

> **One Teaching, One Observing** with one teacher directly instructing students while the other observes students for evidence of learning. **One Teaching, One Assisting** with one teacher directly instructing students while the other assists individual students as needed. **Parallel Teaching** will divide the class into two groups and each teacher teaches the same information at the same time. **Station Teaching** requires each teacher to teach a specific part of the content to different groups as they rotate between teachers. **Alternative Teaching** requires one teacher to teach the bulk of the students, and the other teaches a small group based on need. **Team Teaching** includes both teachers, directly instructing students at the same time –sometimes called "tag team teaching." (para. 2)

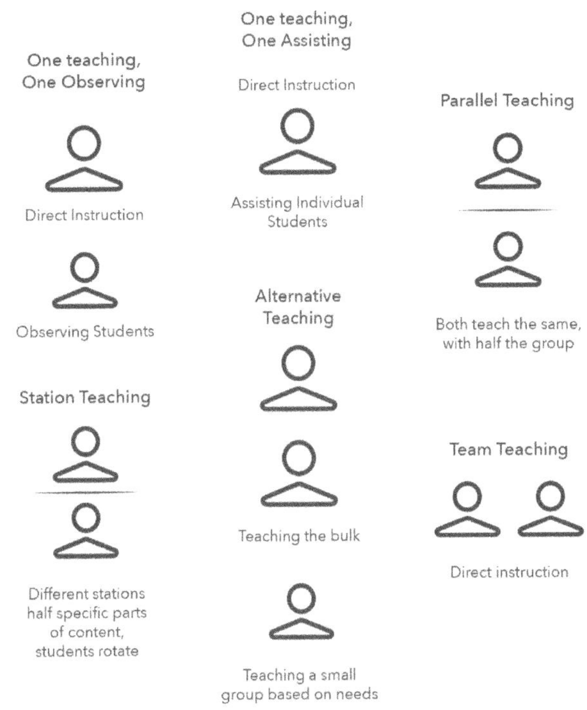

Figure 3.2 Variations on Teaching Teams based on Cassel

Even within these different approaches, different types of relationships with varied outcomes may occur. For example, some schools we have worked with have **master/apprentice** relationships in each classroom, with a variety of results. A common approach is the **student teacher/seasoned educator** pairing common during early service-learning experiences. The best of these pairings are true partnerships where the young educator is encouraged to actively participate and is given opportunities to share insights in real-time. By contrast, we have observed the student teacher sitting passively in the back of the room for 6 weeks, eventually given one brief shining, high-stakes moment to show what they can do while the seasoned educator sits at a desk catching up on grading. We have also witnessed problematic personality conflicts between pairs of educators that emerge early in the pairing and become more intense over time.

Some other examples may consider the **class teacher and the special education teacher** working together in the same classroom to promote an inclusive type of education. Other examples we have experienced are a **class teacher** and **another adult,** external or internal from the same organization, to support students one-on-one with their reading skills. A similar example could be **teachers and conversation language assistants** when learning a second language, with programs such as CAPS (*Conversation Assistant Programme Spain*), or similar types of programs.

Our Experience

Mar experienced being a Spanish conversation language assistant at Xaverian College during her stay in Manchester, England in 2006-7. Years later, she had the pleasure of being accompanied in the classroom by other language assistants from the USA and England in both Pre-primary and Primary, and secondary and high school, while an EFL teacher in Barcelona. Her experience is all about linguistic, cultural and teaching lessons learned thanks to the different types of interactions with each of them.

In some other successful contexts, like High Tech High schools, teacher pairs co-planning and co-teaching have proved to succeed as long as some essential aspects are at stake. Figure 3.3 captures the essence of the fishbone process where the central focus (at the top of the page or the head of the fish) is broken into key elements along the spine and fine details of the bones themselves.

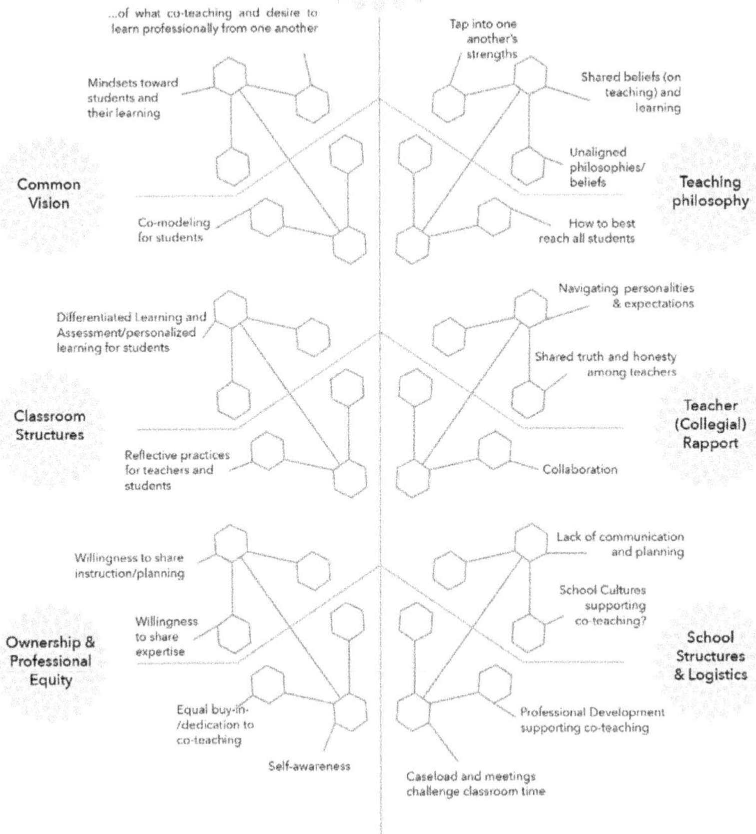

Figure 3.3 Adapted from Fishbone Process based on High Tech High

Trios

Teams of three represent a good starting point for high levels of engagement and accountability, especially if they are mixed-ability and cross-curricular teams. This is why you might consider adding the perspective of special education, world language, or a school counselor to the mix.

As a team of three authors with varied skills and experiences, we have directly experienced the magic and value of working at our maximum potential. Each of us has brought our expertise, knowledge, skills and talents, complementing each other and putting them at the service of a common goal. In fact, we decided to embark on this journey together as a trio, and this is how we have moved forward to achieve our shared aim: the co-writing of this book to enlighten and facilitate teamwork, particularly in the educational field.

Quads

A team of four allows for a variety of skills (eg. communication, creativity, technology) as well as of key learning areas (eg. science, math, language arts, and social studies). For example, they could share responsibility for the same group of 125 middle school learners all together, potentially for two or three consecutive years. Apart from content areas, it also allows for a wide variety of competencies and skills, which are also a key factor.

Five or Six

Grade-level teams of five or six are common in large elementary and middle schools. The larger the group size in any context, the more difficult it can be to schedule common planning time. By contrast, the benefit of larger groups is the potential to include perspectives from people who have worked with learners for multiple years in the realm of art, music, technology, and athletics rather than in year-level key learning areas. Multiple perspectives are not limited to teams of five or six; this can be achieved with pairs, trios, and quads as well.

Seven or more

Teams of seven or more are typically too large and cumbersome to not only schedule common planning time but also to make decisions.

Our experience

Larger groups make it easier to push back from the table, assume others will take on the work and to simply not participate. Every team needs full participation to grow and succeed. This is why breaking large teams into subgroups that share the same goal could work better. In this way, roles can be shared and assigned or distributed, so that every single member takes agency and gets actively engaged. In any case, as long as roles are clearly defined and tasks assigned, larger teams can also succeed.

For instance, this is a common practice within many sports teams, such as offense/defense or infield/outfield. A reason why education should expand beyond the school day with after-school or extracurricular activities, and connect with opportunities beyond the school walls, which may foster collaborative practices from which both learners and educators can benefit.

Larger online team sizes

According to Erickson and Gratton (2007),

> Large teams are often formed to ensure the involvement of a wide stakeholder group, the coordination of a diverse set of activities, and the harnessing of multiple skills. As a consequence, many inevitably involve 100 people or more. However, our research shows that as the size of the team increases beyond 20 members, the level of natural cooperation among members of the team decreases. (p.6)

The world continues to adapt to online communities that typically gather in scheduled settings and perform without real-world, face-to-face interactions that allow participants to read the subtle reactions of team members. How is it possible for these groups to persist? Doesn't their very existence negate the group size discussion above?

YES, AND, BECAUSE. YES, the groups persist, AND the nature of the group work shares some similarities to the face-to-face groups discussed above, BECAUSE online groups interact at several scales. We need to be mindful of the ways they can connect and interact with each other.

For example, a webinar or MOOC (Massive Open Online Course) typically distributes lectures using a shared platform. Now the lecture is available at any time of day, allowing each participant to select the best time to engage with that information and then join in chats, small group "rooms" and other means of discussing and collaborating with their peers anywhere around the world. Ultimately MOOCs, webinars, and conferences employ the same group-size techniques noted above.

An example could be taken from *Inspired Classroom* in Missoula, Montana, which provides online experiences for learners and educators across the United States, combining pre-recorded presentations with live discussions between small groups and content providers.

"I think elementary education is tricky. You have your own classroom and you spend your day from eight to three o'clock with children. And it can often feel lonely in that work when you don't have as much time for adult connection. I have been on several teams where just because you're members of the same grade level doesn't mean that there's companionship, trust, or friendship that develops out of that. I have also been on teams where the opposite is true and your grade-level teammate becomes one of your best friends both inside and outside the school building. At the core, we all want to be on teams where our teammates value our unique contributions and where we help each other outgrow ourselves not only in our instructional moves but in just being better humans."

- Dr. Katie Cunningham, Educator, Author of Start With Joy.
Connecticut, USA (2022)

Team Challenge: Relationships

This exercise is an assessment of current and future age/grade transitions associated with effective learning environments and how many years teaching teams can effectively maintain relationships with the same group of learners. Identify a recorder for your group and note key issues on a large sheet of paper.

GROUP 1:
A.   At what age should we first engage young people in our community?
- *0 1 2 3 4 5?*

B.   How long can you effectively maintain relationships with learners and how is that achieved?
- *2 3 4 5 6 7 8 9 10 11 12 years?*

GROUP 2:
C.   Where are the significant developmental changes that suggest the most appropriate grade groupings within the school?
- *EC PK K 1 2 3 4 5 6 7 8 9 10 11 12 13 14 15 16 17 18 19 20*
- How does the K-6/7-8/9-12 configuration of most of your schools impact forming relationships?

D.   Are there certain groups that should not share spaces and how can we achieve social separation between those groups?

E.   What groups benefit the most from connecting to each other and how can we create those connections?

GROUP 3:
F.   As a teacher, how many young people can you know well (know that a grandparent is ill)?

G.   As a principal, how many young people can you know well (know their name, struggles, and shining moments)? How many teachers do you know well (know they are caring for a sick parent, shine when paired with others)?

H.   How many teachers can work effectively together as a team? What happens when the team is too small or too large?
- *2 3 4 5 6?*

I.   What did we learn from the COVID-19 pandemic about how we might build relationships?

Identify a spokesperson for your group and share the highlights of your discussion with the whole group.

Identify Guiding Principles, for example, "Subdivide the school to support effective teams of 4-5 teachers/staff in small learning communities of less than 150."

Your Turn: What team size is best for you? Why so?

3.2 Types of Teams

Along with the size of the team, the type of team is also relevant and worthy of consideration. For example, teams can be focused on content, coordinating curriculum delivery, cooperatively contributing to a greater whole, or collaborating in real-time with peers. We have encountered several types of teams, which we have organized in alphabetical order; and we suspect that there are many more you can add to this list.

Agile Teams

These self-organized teams are based on teamwork and collective progress, and their essence is on a mindset of experimentation, communication, collaboration, and using principles over practices (Rothman & Kilby, 2019). All these can lead to a socio-psychological environment of high performance. Although created for software development, these types of teams have nowadays increasingly spread widely to other spheres, even to education. You can learn more about this type of teaming, its mindset, and connected methodologies in chapter 5.

AI Teammates

What would happen if you were to invite ChatGPT into your team? You might intentionally use artificial intelligence (AI) to expand upon the ideas your team might develop in greater detail. For example, use AI to generate creative ideas, or lesson planning as a starting point, intentionally requesting 10 different points of view. Other AI teammates might be found in the form of experts, and partners who share their ideas in Youtube videos. Rather than being fearful of AI, we can encourage its usage as a tool or as a supplementary team member, available to us in a digital form.

Central Command

A leader directs subordinates to lead teams of third-tier team members. They are effective in static conditions or processes, including complex ones, with known outcomes. McChrystal (2015) notes that, unfortunately, this is generally not effective in the world of VUCAH (Volatility, Uncertainty, Complexity, Ambiguity, and Hyperconnectivity), as complex conditions dominate our daily experiences.

Collaborative Teams

In business, sports, and educational settings, collaborative teams are created to plan, co-create, deliver, and reflect in both compressed timeframes and in enduring practices. Collaborative teams in education might be formed to create interdisciplinary or cross-curricular projects that require the expertise and perspectives of each teammate. Similar to improvisational jazz, comedy or acting groups, each person shares their strengths and typically builds upon the contributions of their peers based on the 'Yes, and…' principle. A collaborative team sustains focus on a common theme, maintains and builds upon the diversity of the team, and co-creates something greater than the sum of the parts.

In *Teamwork*, Wild, Mayeaux, & Edmonds (2008) note that

> Whether you are fresh out of college or a seasoned veteran, you will find that teamwork provides a powerful foundation for professional collaboration and high achievement. Through teamwork, veterans become energized by the exuberance of new teachers who are bursting with ideas for innovative curricular connections. Novice teachers, in turn, reap the benefits of working with experienced educators who can provide sound advice about instructional pacing, classroom management, and other fundamental skills they've refined over time.

Competitive Teams

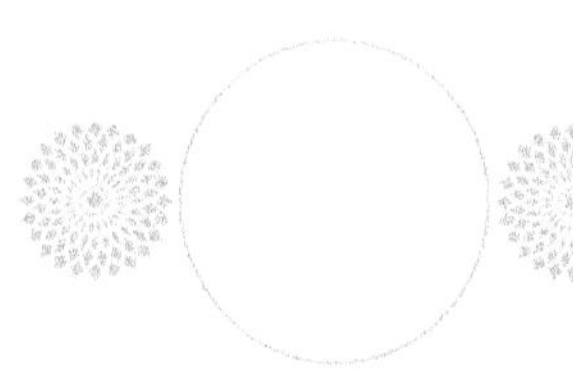

Team members belong to a team with a shared goal to compete against other teams on a specific field. These teams are typically found in sports and athletics, but also in the world of business. Interestingly, research shows that competitive teams succeed through collaboration. For example, two or more teams might be competing in a track and field event, but require collaboration to achieve their goals, such as Mar's relay team in her origin story.

Content Teams

Focused mainly on distributing specific content and information. For example, the early literacy program, the math curriculum, the science department, the social studies the language arts department, world languages department, etc.

Cooperative Teams

Each team member adds their component on the assembly line, including dividing the work between specialists or planning as an interdisciplinary team but delivering asynchronously.

> *Additional Resources*
>
> *An extended cooperative learning practice in education is the so-called 'jigsaw classroom', invented and developed in the early 1970s by Elliot Aronson and his students at the University of Texas and the University of California. With this practice, students cooperate by moving back and forth from jigsaw to expert groups. (Berger, et al., 2020)*

Coordinated Teams

Developing a common effort, delivery, and assessment. For example, the Middle School Experience or Year 9 transition, pedagogical teams, student intervention, department heads, curriculum-development teams, etc.

Crew Teams

EL (formerly Expeditionary Learning) schools place a particular emphasis on creating a culture of teamwork with a focus on social-emotional well-being and redefining success as a combination of personal best and collective effort. Crew Teams co-create group expectations for learners, educators, and community partners, sharing different types of experiences, making agreements visible and integrated with learning, at the same time that they put values into action to make the world a better place.

In the book *We Are Crew*, Ron Berger, Anne Vilen and Libby Woodfin

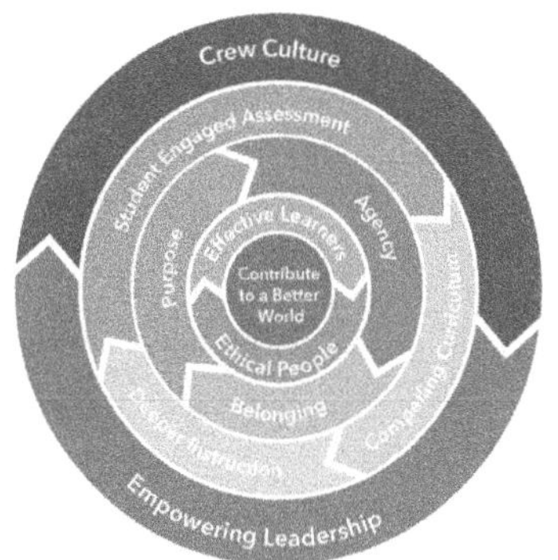

(2020) share numerous examples of how EL schools develop a culture of Crew- a place where staff "respect each other, support each other and work together as a team" (p. 12). Each member of the Crew makes "the commitment to know each other well and understand each other's perspectives" (Berger et al., 2020 p. 12). "Crew culture involves all students and all staff" in all settings.

Figure 3.4 Crew Teams, Based on We Are Crew

Hybrid Teams

Groups of people working together synchronously, partly remotely and partly in-person, with a shared purpose. Although generally they were born out of necessity due to the pandemic, this type of organization remains relevant post-pandemic as it opens up possibilities for more engaging educational activities (Cheng Jie Lee et al., 2022, p. 701). Also, this type of organization allows more inclusive opportunities for learners' participation from a distance and respecting their preferred ways of engagement bearing in mind the Universal Design for Learning (UDL) approach.

Interdisciplinary Teams

A value of the integrated learning/interdisciplinary team is that we see young people from different perspectives, and as a result, see young people more holistically.

Sporadic Teams

Created in spaces like professional development workshops, where educators or others are encouraged to become part of a team for a specific purpose for a very short period of time. Examples include one-day workshops, hackathons, Edcamps, Edhacks, Bootcamps, etc.

The Tribe

If we think about educational environments, the tribe could be a whole institution or organization, a section in a school (Pre-primary/Junior School, Primary/Middle School, Secondary/High School, Higher Education, Vocational training), a group of educators in a whole learning environment, etc. In the end, shouldn't it be about sharing a set of values and beliefs concerning education and learning? According to Sinek, Mead, and Docker (2017)ʼ the tribe can be understood as

> "any group of people who come together around a common set of values and beliefs. A tribe can be an entire organization or a small team. Often, where you sit within the organization determines who you view as your tribe. If you are the CEO of an organization, everyone who works within the organization is your tribe. If you are the director of a division, the people who work in your division are the members of your tribe. If you are the leader or member of a team, the team is your tribe. If your organization's structure isn't so clearly defined, rely on what feels right. It's possible that a team member may fit into more than one tribe. The bottom line is a tribe is the place where you feel you belong." (p. 64)

We are aware of the connotations that the word tribe may have in different places all over the world. Here we want to acknowledge any misleading historical and cultural assumptions this concept may be attached to, as well as to dismantle all racial stereotypes that may have been imposed for centuries. At the same time, we would like to shed light on the positive essence of this term, as it contains intrinsic values that may enhance the sense of community, belonging, and shared values and beliefs within any collective, and therefore, within any team.

Ubuntu Teams

The familiar description of ubuntu, "I am because we are" is occasionally completed with the phrase, "and we are because I am."

How might this cycle of connection and contribution impact the creation of an ubuntu team? An ubuntu team might focus on sustaining empathetic communication between individuals and the collective with a service-oriented approach to impact the broader community. Also, it may nurture a deep sense of interconnectedness, shared responsibility, and mutual respect by creating an inclusive and supportive environment, where decisions are made in consensus and leadership is distributed and shared among the members. An ubuntu team might focus on questions such as "How does the collective shape, but not define the individual?" and "How does each individual shape, but not define the collective?" As an ubuntu team develops over time, new questions are likely to emerge.

Virtual Teams

Groups of learners working together remotely, asynchronously or synchronously, with a shared purpose. We can learn more about them from the industry and business fields. According to Powell, Piccoli & Ives (2004), these are defined as "groups of geographically, organizationally and/or time dispersed workers brought together by information and telecommunication technologies to accomplish one or more organizational tasks." (p. 7)

In the educational field, we saw how the pandemic encouraged, and even forced, the creation of virtual groups, and hopefully, virtual teams too. Although it was very challenging for many educators and learners across the globe especially in the beginning, it also allowed for new opportunities to emerge. Besides, these can bring added value, as we can foster transnational and cross-cultural virtual collaboration among learners and educators from all over the world. As Ferris and Godar (2006) point out, "To educators, one of the most exciting potential uses of the Internet can be to enable students from different countries to exchange information and come to know one another and each another's culture" (p. xi).

An aside about professional learning communities
Nick has spent time observing Professional Learning Communities (PLC's) or Professional Learning Teams (PLT's) in practice and suspects that many school leaders simply renamed the "Math Department" the "Math PLC," carved out time in the timetable for the PLC to work together and called it good. Try as they might, it is unlikely that those 4-8 educators will ever share the same learners at the same point in time. A secondary school math team is typically specialized into those who focus on algebra, geometry, trigonometry, and calculus. The teaching of math is the primary passion of those educators, each following a particular scope and sequence important to the geometry teacher who hands off a group of learners to the trigonometry educator next year, knowing that learners were adequately prepared.

*The most effective PLC's are **interdisciplinary teams**, meeting daily in a quick triage to review which students are shining, which are struggling, and which are treading water. The second focus of an effective PLC is on the development of interdisciplinary projects, a third focus would be content mastery. Math, science, language arts, and social studies educators may need to meet once a month by discipline for a tune-up and once a year to look at changes to the curriculum. But we can think of no reason why content-focused teams would need to meet every day in a world where varied perspectives on learners are crucial to the success of each young person.*

A quick example. We know young people who thrive in the world of science but struggle with basic communication skills. If we continue to work in silos rather than relationship-based teams, a science educator may see great potential in the same student the language arts educator views as disengaged. When those two educators connect and share insights a more complete picture of the learner is revealed, and perhaps a new strategy allows the struggling learner to express what they are learning in science in language arts or using world language to research and express issues in social studies.

3.3 Number and Your Team(s)

YES, AND, BECAUSE. In a typical American school, an educator may be on several teams, each with different expectations and timeframes. For instance, team #1 might be a **Collaborative Team** within a small learning community with a relationship focused on knowing every learner and coaching interdisciplinary projects with personal, cultural, local or global relevance. This team meets every day. Team #2 might be a **Coordinated Team** which includes the **Collaborative Team** as well as art, Music, CTE, and Physical Education. This team might meet monthly to coordinate planning and delivery efforts between **Collaborative Teams**. Team #3 could be a **Content Team** with a focus on the continuity of the Math or Science curriculum. This team might meet once a term or once a year.

This can also be the case in other countries around the world. In Mar's particular experience in Spanish schools, she has been involved in teams with different purposes in a school environment: the foreign languages department, the pedagogical team, the school innovation team, and the coordination team for a Network of Innovation. And all that, at the same time!

In the dynamic landscape of higher education, Erin often finds herself navigating multiple team environments simultaneously as a student, faculty member, expert, and community member. This multifaceted engagement can span departmental committees, interdisciplinary research groups, and even external partnerships.

The work is diverse yet always aligned with her vision as a professional educator. Her vision and mission are what tether her to the work that each team may ask of her. Ranging from teams focused on clinical experiences, curriculum, scholarships, faculty evaluations, admissions, Diversity, Equity, and Inclusion, graduate thesis, and presentations to state and national organizations.

In some settings she has wisdom to share, in others, she is accelerating awareness. She is able to leverage her expertise in varied contexts, fostering innovation and cross-pollination of ideas. Involvement like this not only enriches her professional experience but also contributes to the institution's overall agility and responsiveness to emerging challenges. It does require a delicate balancing act, as she must manage competing priorities, different team cultures, and potentially conflicting expectations. In order to do this, she relies on her strong communication skills, adaptability, and a keen sense of time management. Serving as a connector and bridge builder between committees, departments, and disciplines.

As an educational consultant Nick often finds himself working in numerous teams at the same time, often in very different roles. For example, Fundación Paraguaya trained Nick and Kavita Tanna how to use the Stoplight community engagement tool. In that setting, they were active learners with many seasoned partners supporting them. The sessions were developed in English and Spanish, which placed each of them in teams of bilingual, English-only and Spanish-only teams. Ultimately, the work has been extended to communities in Kenya, Nigeria, Zimbabwe, Nepal and Australia, where individuals and families form teams to identify their strengths and challenges.

Your Team(s):

What is your diagram?
Stop and think about the team size and the types of teams you are or have been involved in. Create your own web or network, a list, a mind map, a visual thinking organizer, or any other type of representation you prefer. invest some time thinking about what the benefits and the drawbacks are for each of them. Finally, we encourage you to think about your top 3 takeaways.

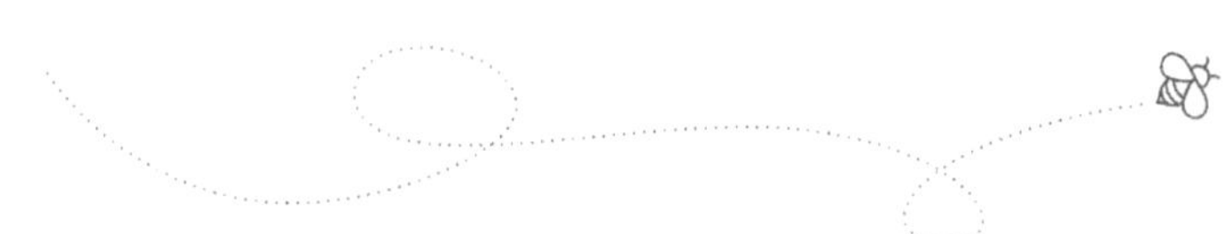

You have achieved the Goldilocks size of your team — not too small, not too large. Just right. With that confidence in the size of your team, you also have had opportunities to think about the type of team you have created. Both of these choices are important as you take up the next phase of your work: growing as a team, facing challenges, and making decisions together.

CHAPTER 4: TEAMWORK STRATEGIES

A deep and rich toolbox of strategies makes all the difference.

"If you want to lift yourself up, lift up someone else."
                    - Booker T. Washington, Educator & Author. Tuskegee, Alabama

Simple team decisions about when to meet, how often to meet, and how long to meet build confidence in tackling complex challenges every team will face.

This chapter will help you to create and expand a toolbox full of teamwork tools that you can use, combine, or modify for future situations. There is not one single strategy, but multiple strategies generating exponential combinations.

In our experience in multiple and diverse teams, we know that teamwork goes through different stages and that the more strategies you have in your **teamwork toolbox,** the easier it is for each of you to work collaboratively within any team.

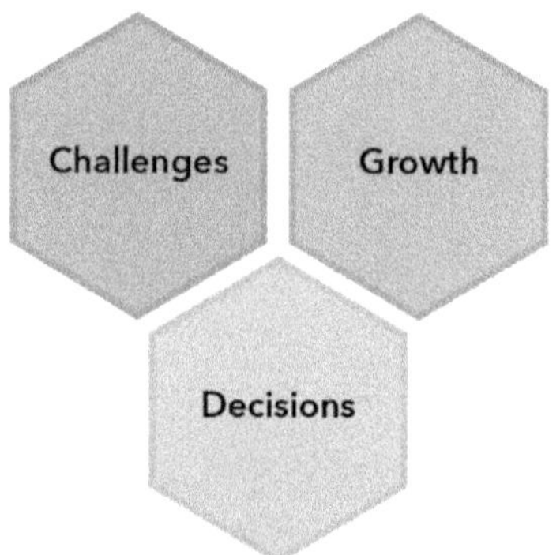

In this chapter, we have gathered teamwork strategies to walk through those different stages mindfully and successfully. They can be helpful for learners, educators, and school and learning leaders independently of their educational and learning environment. To make the most of the implementation of these strategies, we encourage you to count on your critical thinking skills, and, to decide if, and when, you want to use them following the instructions that we suggest step by step, or if you prefer to adapt and adjust them to your context. We are aware that a strategy that may work with one team, may not work so well with another one. We need to learn how to read each team in its individuality and to tune these strategies according to both the composition of each team, and the specific stage they are going through.

First, consider the strategies you have used so far. More importantly, reflect on how effective they have been, what advantages and drawbacks you found, and which ones, and why, have proven to be the most successful ones for you as a member of different kinds of teams. Of course, there is no need to do everything by yourself, what if you reflect on these questions with your team as well?

__Your Turn:__ Invest some time thinking about strategies you may be using or have used in any team you can think of. Which categories would you classify them into? Take your notes here.

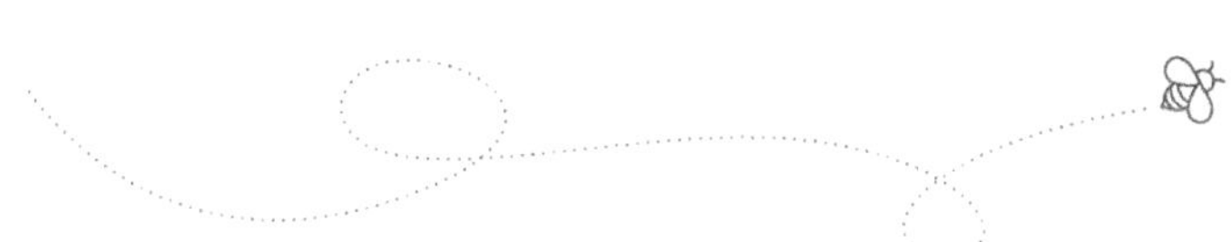

This robust **teamwork strategy toolbox** may help us become more agile, build the most positive and safe atmosphere, communicate effectively to face challenges, make the most suitable decisions we can consider at a specific moment in a particular situation, and solve problems. This is why we decided to classify them into three main categories: Positive Growth Strategies, Flowing with Challenges, and Decision-Making.

When thinking about which strategies could be valuable to add to this toolbox, the three of us brought our experience of incorporating strategies and techniques from different fields. For example, Mar brought her passion for improvisation to improve her public speaking, creative, and collaborative skills. She routinely draws upon many sources which have proved to be helpful when boosting different strategies through improvisation. As Alfie Kohn (2011) notes,

> the best kind of learning experience in English, math or any other subject doesn't feel like a chamber music piece, it feels more like a jazz improvisation.

Our experience is that great teaching and learning looks and feels a lot like improvisation. We take what is offered, build upon it, and face real challenges in our team, organization, community, and the world. These improvisation skills are implemented in our teaching and learning, rather than reading from a daily script. Yet, we are also aware that in some institutions a very detailed plan based on the curriculum needs to be followed from A to Z. Let's see this from another angle, as an opportunity. What if that plan included some of these improv techniques, which enrich teamwork and boost a wide variety of skills in multiple ways?

Yes, and... Great educators are a bit like camp counselors, able to read the energy of the room and know when to change up the approach.

Yes, and… Even more, improvisation has a lot to offer to education when it comes to collaboration, communication, and creativity! Improvisation is a crucial way to help participants "build effective teams, break down silos, foster creativity, and spark innovation." (Leonard & Yorton, 2015, p.4)

4.1. Strategies for Positive Team Growth

In 2023, we worked with a community in the United States that was initiating team teaching in five middle schools. As we noted in the introduction, the 3,000 young people in these five schools cannot wait 5-6 years for the adults to form highly effective teams. Teams will need to be capable of meeting their wide range of needs during a time of accelerated physical, social, emotional, and intellectual change.

The annotated agenda below illustrates the flow of experiences designed to rapidly build the capacity to work as a team. Participants typically leave this professional learning experience with clarity of purpose and commit to meaningful next steps that can be implemented quickly.

Team Challenge: One Day Workshop
PREPARATION
- o What words and images draw participants to gather?
- o Space to move, make learning visible
- o Large notepads, markers, sticky notes, dots

8:30-8:45 WELCOME: DOING/ CURIOUS/ SUCCESS © Catalyst Learning Labs
- o How are you doing?
- o What are you curious about?
- o What would success look like for you?
- o Curiosity on one sticky note color/ Success on other
- o Each table identifies a Recorder (Red), Reporter (Amber) and Reflector (Green) for each exercise (using dots to identify role). Recorder organizes sticky notes. Reflector adds a big insight.
- o Share at each table, one table invited to share with the whole group, second or third table to add something new. Reporter places large sheet of paper/ sticky notes on an adjacent wall.

8:45-9:15 NAME ORIGIN STORY © Globally Reconnect
- o Each person shares the origins of their name.
- o Recorder, Reporter, Reflector
- o Share at each table, share with whole group.

9:15-10:00 MOST POWERFUL LEARNING EXPERIENCE
- o Each person shares their most powerful learning experience using prompts of when, where, who, what, how.
- o Recorder, Reporter, Reflector
- o Share at each table, share with whole group.

10:00-10:15 PURPOSEFUL BREAK
- o Dance? Music? Movement? Gallery Walk?

10:15-11:00 ACRONYM IMPROV © Collaborative Learning Network
- o Whole group quickly identifies education acronyms.
- o Each group has 5 minutes to create a simple message.
- o Each group has 2-3 minutes to achieve a mike-drop moment, take a bow and open the stage for the next group.

11:00-12:00 TED TALK TRIO IMPROV © Collaborative Learning Network
- o 5 minutes to create a simple, multi-generational tale of failure, recovery and persistence.
- o Achieve a poignant, shared story of collaboration.

- o Each group has 2-3 minutes to achieve a mike-drop moment, take a bow and open the stage for the next group.

12:00-1:00 SLOW LUNCH
- o Set tables
- o Make and eat meal together

1:00-1:05 teamED Tool © *teamED*
- o Whole group identifies 6-8 skills a team of educators need to be successful: Advisory, SEL, Relationships, Time Management, Technology Integration, Community Partnerships, Content Mastery, Cross-Curricular Experiences.

1:05-1:45 teamED Tool © *teamED*
- o Brief overview of the model.
- o Fill the left-hand column of a pre-printed diagram.
- o Circle, Triangle, Square, Star, Diamond

1:45-2:00 ADVENTURE BREAK
- o Adventure/Challenge
- o Lead the team from behind through a simple obstacle course.

2:00-2:45 JIGSAW APPLICATION © *Globally Reconnect/ Collaborative Learning Network*
- o How might we use this tool to create effective teams of young people working on shared projects?
- o How might we work as a team to create an integrated learning experience?
- o How might we use this tool to teach together?

2:45-3:00 SHARE
- o Recorder, Reporter, Reflector
- o Share at each table, share with the whole group.

3:00-3:05 LOGISTICS/NEXT STEPS
- o Facilitators share any BRIEF Logistics/Next Steps.

3:05-3:20 SURPRISE/DELIGHT/WONDER © *Catalyst Learning Labs*
- o Recorder, Reporter, Reflector
- o Share at each table, share with the whole group.

3:20-3:30 CLOSING WITH FEELING © *Catalyst Learning Labs*
- o Recorder, Reporter, Reflector
- o Share at each table, share with the whole group.

Other Voices:
Feedback from a February 2024 workshop introducing the teamED framework

"I was surprised how much I learned about others in the room in such a short period of time"

"I was surprised to learn about each other and see how closely connected we are."

"I was delighted to be learning together, to lead together"

"I wonder how today will shape future interactions."

"I wonder how we can spread learning & success from today within our district."

"I wonder if we can do this with staff and build a more trustworthy team?"

4.1.1. Communicating, Sharing & Celebrating Strategies

1) Effective Communication

The following strategies begin with developing our listening skills while moving toward active dialogue.

1, 2, 3 Listen

When being part of a team, we often discover that one person loves taking the lead and speaks, speaks, and speaks… Do we want only one voice to be heard? Or shall we offer opportunities to hear from everyone? This particular active listening and speaking strategy is very practical, especially if you want to create an atmosphere of equity and make sure everybody has their turn to speak for the same amount of time. Or at least, that everyone is offered the same amount of time and they can use it as they prefer, fully or just to agree and then keep silent.

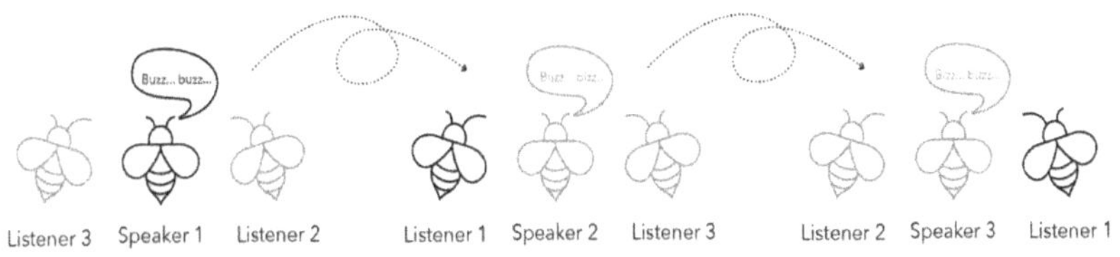

To start with, speakers can assign themselves their roles as speakers 1,2 & 3. Ask speakers to take turns speaking to the two listeners. Set a timer. When members perform as listeners, ask them to hold space in silence and put all their attention on the speaker, so that they can build upon their ideas if they take the second turn. As speakers, they can speak as much as they like during the period of time equally assigned. Learning to respect each member's turn is also a lesson to learn.

Voice Mirror

A good way to be present and make sure that active listening is effective is to put the 'voice mirror' technique into practice. It is a simple but challenging practice, which requires awareness and constant practice. Yet, it can make a positive difference in the way we communicate with others.

This strategy includes repeating the words a speaker is saying silently in our minds, so as to follow the thread and not react immediately with our own reply. Thus, we prevent our reactive speech from going over the other person's speech. This is what is referred to as listening-to-understand, instead of listening-to-respond. As Steven Covey (2004) said: "most people do not listen with the intent to understand; they listen with the intent to reply." (p. 239). The voice mirror helps teammates to deepen their understanding of each other.

Speaker 1   Listener 1

SLANT

Another useful strategy to use when communicating is the SLANT listening technique; an acronym that reminds learners to focus. It both enhances active listening and also encourages positive non-verbal behavior.

Sit up
Listen
Ask and answer questions
Nod your head
Track the speaker

It's shorthand to remind students either about the "S" in SLANT or about the whole thing ("Make sure you are SLANTing.") It helps to use nonverbal signals (pointing to your eyes with your two fingers to remind a student to track) to avoid interrupting your instruction (Lemov, 2010)

Inspiring Video

Although Lemov tells us about SLANT in the students and classroom setting, try it in different teams as a basic starting point to becoming primarily aware of the listener role in any communication setting.

Other Voices

"Working in a school, there are so many people and so many different perspectives to consider when decisions are made. And that requires input from everybody. And lots of different voices, whether that's the students voice, voices from parents, voices from other teaching colleagues, or people in administrative types of roles, this work requires everyone to have a voice for it to work."
- Louise Whitaker, Primary School Educator,
Macquarie College. Wallsend, Australia. (2020)

Reflective Dialogue

Eight norms have been identified for each person to understand, agree upon, adopt, monitor, and assess when working as a facilitating and contributing member of a team (Baker, Costa & Shalit, 1997; Garmston & Wellman, 1999):
1. pausing
2. paraphrasing
3. probing and clarifying
4. putting your ideas on and pulling them off the table
5. paying attention to oneself and others
6. presuming positive intentionality and positive presuppositions
7. providing data
8. pursuing a balance between advocacy and inquiry

This challenge builds upon the elements of Reflective Dialogue noted above.

Participants first role-play a fictional decision-making challenge typically found within learning communities, followed by a facilitated decision-making process for a local issue and conclude in participant-led use of the decision-making process for a pressing concern.

The facilitator summarizes the challenge and asks what the group would recommend. For example: how might the dining experience make a positive contribution to learning? Leave at least 30 seconds before anyone in the group speaks. Leave at least 30 seconds before the next person speaks. Periodically, the facilitator summarizes the contributions of the group in the form of a question- "Am I hearing that we could…?" Repeat at least three times, maybe more.

If you are having a hard time letting enough time go by before someone else speaks reflect on these questions before speaking:
- *What did the last speaker say?*
- *What was the most important thing to me that they just shared?*
- *What do I think about what was shared?*
- *What new insights do I have to contribute?*
- *Do I have anything to share?*

Or consider the acronym WAIT: Why Am I Talking? or THINK: True, Helpful, Inspiring, Necessary, Kind

(photo by Nick Salmon)

Think-Pair-Share

This visible thinking routine enhances communication and encourages everyone to think about a topic, pair with a peer, and then share their thoughts (Project Zero, 2015).

Start with an individual reflection. No spoken words. You can either simply keep your thoughts in your mind or capture one idea per sticky note. Pair with another team member. Share with that person.

Then you can share with your small group. When sharing in a small group, always share your partner's ideas (with their permission), not your own. In this way, we are enhancing active listening skills. When these basic rules are understood, each participant has the opportunity to be more attentive to what their partner is sharing. It helps to tamp down the out-sized egos and allows every voice to be heard.

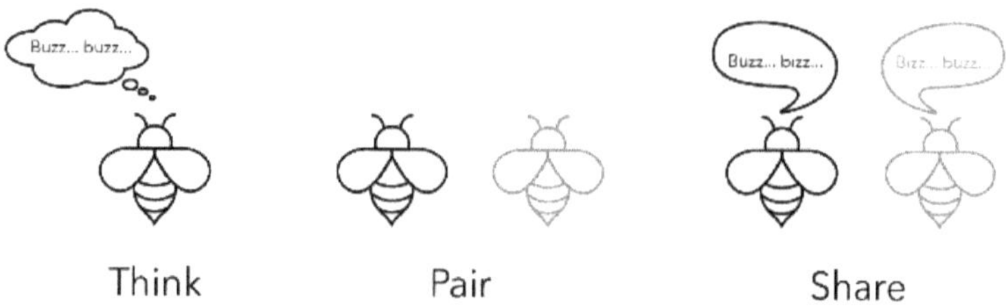

Think   Pair   Share

Team Challenge: Natural Timers: Fire, Water and Sound
These three challenges offer opportunities to use natural timers of fire, water, and sound to release your team from the distraction of a ticking timer or countdown timer. Feel free to use natural elements to manage/assign time to each speaker so that the time flows more naturally.

Match Timer
How about lighting matches? Yes, real matches! If you want a more random and exciting strategy to get started with a new team, try it! And feel free to come up with other original varieties that you easily adapt to the context you are in.

Every person is given a match, and they can speak as long as their match is lit, one at a time. This technique can be applied when we know there is a safe space and responsible people. We don't want anyone to get burned! We just want to bring excitement and creativity into the new team from the very beginning.

Moreover, it's not only about lighting the match that can be exciting for the team but also about what makes a powerful fire-starter. For instance, using a question or 'fill-in-the-blank' are two common and powerful fire-starters (Gray, Brown & Macanufo, 2010, p. 17)

Pebbles in Water
Each person in a conversation is given a pebble (or three). Drop a pebble in a large bowl of water. Watch the ripples on the surface of the water until they dissipate and the water becomes still. Once this has occurred, the next speaker may begin, or they may drop their pebble in the water resulting in a prolonged period of silence.

Sound a Gong
This same technique can be achieved using a gong or bowl, allowing the sound to dissipate before the next speaker. You may be surprised how long a tone remains audible to each individual, and how quickly the team adjusts their speaking patterns to wait for each tone to complete the cycle.

Be impeccable with your words

In *The Four Agreements*, Don Miguel Ruiz (2018) suggested, "Be impeccable with your words" as the first agreement; a good reminder to be mindful of the words we use and the power each word has. It can be embraced along with the other three agreements to get its fullest potential:

> 2. Don't Take Anything Personally
> 3. Don't Make Assumptions
> 4. Always Do Your Best

How useful could this be in your daily life, when talking to anyone in your team, or even to anyone who may not even know you? And why not put the four agreements together into practice for a better experience in our interactions to avoid misunderstandings and to make our communication more easy-going?

2) Empathic Growth Strategies

As you and your team utilize the techniques in the prior section, you will build confidence in your speaking and listening skills and your ability to work together as a team. This section focuses on the development of growth strategies for positive teams.

Rotating Roles

Group dynamics are enhanced when roles are shared, rather than the person with the best handwriting taking on the role of recorder; the most vocal person claiming the role of reporter; and the second-most introverted person agreeing to be the reflector (the most introverted person finds other ways to contribute, but often does not take on a more public role). For each exercise or each meeting, we find that rotating through these roles improves communication and leads to deeper insights. We like creating badges (like in scouting) for taking on the roles of recorder, reporter, and reflector. Why so? To make each role visible, and to allow groups to see who has earned their badge and will need to step aside to allow others to grow.

Start by assigning simple roles of recorder, reporter, and reflector and rotate through them from exercise to exercise or meeting to meeting. These roles can be acknowledged with a simple badge, or adding a red, amber, and green dot to your name tag as you take on each role.

Let's consider another possible scenario.
For learners working on a project, initially assigning roles such as actor, director, and videographer can help build confidence. You can spin a hand-made or digital dial and randomly reassign the roles throughout a project to again allow each person to experience each role and see the project from a new perspective.

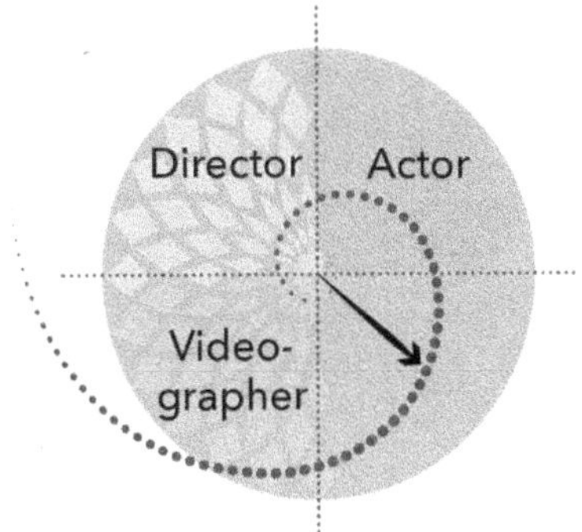

An even more revolutionary practice is to have a group work on a project for 2-3 weeks and then hand their work off to another group. This approach raises the expectations of what a group needs to do before handing over their work and allows less-developed ideas to be given a new look and for well-developed ideas to be handed to groups that may be struggling to express what they know.

Feedback: Kind, Specific and Helpful

Providing powerful feedback among learners, educators, and even community partners may contribute to making progress toward a team's goal. For it to be effective, it must be kind, specific, and helpful, as Ron Berger, founder of Expeditionary Learning, affirms.

Also, it should answer 3 questions:
1) Where are we going? (feed-up),
2) How are we going? (feedback), and
3) Where to next? (feed-forward).
This way we are promoting thinking and actions based on the model of powerful feedback proposed by Hattie and Temperly (2007).

Other forms of feedback follow a similar three-step process, such as "I see, I think, I wonder", from Project Zero or the "What Works? What Could Be Better? and What's Missing?" framework of the Collaborative Learning Network. Each of these triads can be used by young people, peers, educators, and community partners when evaluating the products of a learning journey.

Rather than immediately jumping to providing your insights, you can extend the ideas of others by asking follow-up questions. Suzie Boss captured the "go to" responses to learner questions developed by Newburn that do not include providing an answer but extend the inquiry and curiosity of the young person (Boss & Larmer, 2018, p. 115).

- Can you tell me more about that?
- Can you give me an example?
- Why do you think that?
- I want to hear more of your thinking behind what you are saying
- What's your claim?
- How does that evidence support your reasoning?

These and other lines of inquiry can help individuals and teams develop a new perspective on their collective enterprise. The example on the next page from Ela Ben-Ur illustrates a thoughtful approach to supporting a group that may consistently return to past solutions to new challenges or become stuck in unhelpful patterns of decision-making.

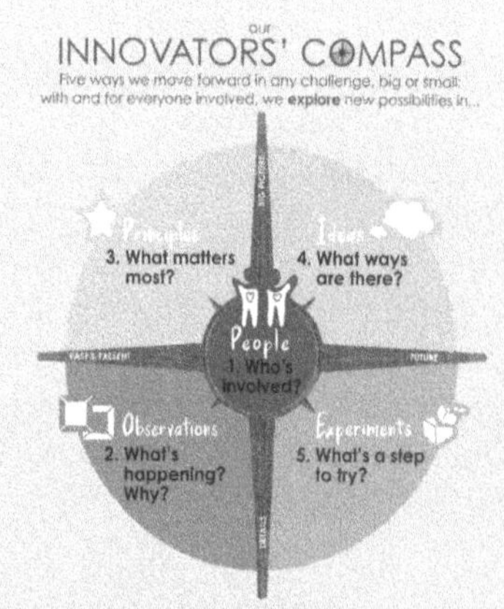

Showing Gratitude

> *I'm grateful that you offered to help me with my project, even though it meant sacrificing some of your free time. (Rowell, 2023, para. 13)*

Even if we understand gratitude either as an enduring disposition, virtue, or affective trait (McCullough & Tsang, 2002; Roberts, 2004) or a temporary emotional state (Fredrickson, 2004, p. 146) experiencing and expressing it improves well-being and nurtures relationships (Rowell, 2023). Practicing how it works in two directions, as a giver and a receiver, will strengthen the bonds within your team while boosting individual psychological well-being.

Apart from its benefits on individuals' physical and mental health, the greatest value lies in its social benefits since it plays a role as "social glue" (Allen, 2018, p. 5) It boosts prosocial behavior by increasing feelings of social worth and enabling individuals to feel socially valued (Grant & Gino, 2010).

A practical way to do it is following the four essential components of the gratitude experience which psychologist Andrea Hussong and her team identified: notice, think, feel, and do. Everyone in your team can work through these prompts.

Also, you can start to practice by giving people compliments. This can raise your emotional awareness and create better relationships with others by noticing things that they do well and telling them how great they are at achieving those particular needs of the group.

Celebrating Milestones

Sit together. Stop and think about your achievements. Appraise. Recognize. Acknowledge. Give credit. Celebrate! And keep moving forward, one win at a time.

Celebrating big or small wins daily, weekly, or whenever your team agrees, is a practice that enhances social positive support. By doing it, you will all build positive emotions both for yourself and for your team. Through experiences of positive emotions, each team member may transform themselves with an upbeat mood, increased motivation, and more engagement. You may become more creative, more resilient, more socially integrated, and more knowledgeable.

Positive emotions of this kind enhance broad thinking, offer more personal resources, nurture resilience, and contribute to better problem-solving and facing challenges. Celebrating milestones also helps reinforce positive behaviors and attitudes, and provides opportunities to strengthen bonds with your teammates, as positive memories of past accomplishments can help motivate people to pursue future goals (Maryville University, n.d.).

Here when we talk about celebrating milestones, we are not just referring to celebrating academic wins, or end products to show publicly to the wider educational community. It is more about celebrating small wins throughout the process of learning, rather than just at the very end. Keeping the team motivated to continue learning and moving forward to achieve the shared goals is an essential practice for team growth. This celebration can target effort, personal development and growth, problem-solving, and even failures as growth opportunities. Celebrating failures can add to the authenticity of a team, and models practices that might be adopted by others. Teams who celebrate failure as well as success are visibly committed to learning, rather than presenting an illusion of constant success. So, let's ensure we make bigger goals more easily achievable by breaking them down into specific, measurable and achievable ones, which end up in tangible advancements (Ciuta, 2023)

In any case, celebrating should consider both individual and team accomplishments. Each single team member needs to feel appraised and recognized. Appraisal and recognition may come in different forms and shapes. One member may just feel touched by a verbal compliment, whereas another may feel rewarded with a dark chocolate bar, or a big round of applause... Why not? As a team, agree on what, why, how, where and when those celebrations will take place.

According to neuroscience research, the most effective form of recognition is public ovation as it triggers the release of both dopamine and oxytocin. Particularly, "ovation that is unexpected, public, tangible, personal, close in time to the goal being met, and comes from peers has the most powerful effect on brain and behavior." (Zak, 2018, p.49) Therefore, think about the types of recognition and celebrations that build your desired team culture.

4.1.2. Creating, Playing, Laughing & Improvising Together

A joyful way of building team cohesion is to step away from the focus on work and engage in creating, playing, laughing, and improvisation. Through this play, enduring social connections and support are formed (Fredrickson, 2004b). Creating meals together can incorporate play, laughter, and improvisation as a menu is created, ingredients are gathered, food is prepared and conversations flow. We can also spend time together doing yoga or mindful breathing. The brain's response to these experiences is proven to build group cohesion. (Sinek, 2014). The following sections include many approaches to changing the collective energy of your team through co-creating, playing, laughing, improvising, and adventuring together.

1) Improvisation

When participating in theatrical improvisation, adults are responsive to one another and build on each other's contribution. Improv is an adult activity which requires that the players work together rather than focusing on their own individual ideas, goals, or egos. It assumes a commitment to the whole rather than on the particular. When an improv troupe is working well together, what they create collectively is greater than the sum of their individual ideas. (Lobman, 2005, p. 306-307)

The following improv examples are ideas to put into practice with your team. Depending on the nature of your team, consider starting small to build confidence in a safe atmosphere, and then move towards more challenging activities.

Rotating Story: *One-Word Story*

All the members of a team gather in a circle and are asked to tell an original story using the following instructions: each member needs to contribute only one word at a time towards the common goal, which is telling the overall narrative. It might be a good practice, especially for members who are used to working in silos. It is remarkable to remember that, "individual participants affirm and build in their unique way to a far more interesting story than they probably would have come up with on their own" (Leonard & Yorton, 2015, p. 43).

Talk Without I

This exercise involves pairing up the members of a group to have a conversation about any topic with the simple rule of not using the first person, "I" (Leonard and Yorton, 2015, pp. 58-59). The focus is not on the conversation itself, but on speaking without I. The purpose is to recognize how each member filters information through their own perspectives when sharing ideas, feedback, or recommendations. In this way, the members learn to frame things in a more accessible and understandable way to their team members, as it is other-directed. After the exercise, Leonard and Yorton suggest investing some time to talk about how each of them can be more conscious of their own point of view.

Yes, And…

Yes, And is one of the foundational elements of improvisation. This may seem a simple expression to accept what a member offers and to add to it; however, by building the scene, one brick at a time (rather than an entire cathedral), it can actually encourage teams to communicate generously and collaboratively and to look for ways to reach an agreement (Leonard & Yorton, 2015). Moreover, it "makes everyone feel heard and respected, and when you have mutual respect, it's possible to work through any performance [or daily educational] challenge" (Leonard & Yorton, 2015, p. 30). Consequently, it can help avoid a single member monopolizing any conversation, situation, or decision.

A 'Yes, And' mindset can enhance interpersonal and team communications, boost the generation, and the development of ideas and initiatives, problem-solving, and conflict resolution.

Once the team has built confidence in 'Yes, Anding', the next step would be to employ the improv tenet "Yes, And, Explore and Heighten", which also lets you build something of interest and weight together (Leonard & Yorton, 2015, p. 40).

2) Escape room experience

Consider taking on the challenges of an **escape room**, in person, or even virtually. This collaborative experience is a powerful activity to go through with your team to boost team building. Pan, Lo, and Neustaedter (2017) state that in real-life escape rooms,

> team members move between loosely and tightly coupled group work and can practice methods to smoothly do so; they can practice gathering situational and workspace awareness; they can practice their communication skills; and, they can practice the development of a shared mental model. (p. 1361)

Moreover, expert creators of this experience argue that this activity can enhance team building because it makes great memories; improves decision-making capabilities; is affordable, but effective; helps to realize natural team leaders, develops task and time management skills; fosters creativity and problem-solving; identifies each member's strengths; supports collaboration; improves communication; and improves team spirit and motivation (Other World Escapes, 2021). In addition, there is already some research in the educational field that has proved "the value of the escape room in encouraging teamwork, facilitating communication, and promoting interprofessionalism" (Friedrich et al., 2019, p. 573).

If you have not tried the experience yourself yet, why not give it a go? All of these experiences represent opportunities to be vulnerable with your teammates as shared in *Getting Naked* by Patrick Lencioni (2020) and in the research of Brené Brown (2020).

The next section includes many of our favorite ways to build trust, common purpose, and deeper communication in your team.

4.1.3. Becoming Actively Connected

In our work with teams around the world, becoming actively connected through eating, dancing, singing, and adventuring provides opportunities to extend the connection beyond sharing powerful stories, learning to listen to each other, and developing collaborative skills. Just as workshops and learning experiences benefit from power poses, brain breaks, and movement, teams can take advantage of a change of venue.

1) Growing & Preparing Food: Eating Together

The benefit of growing and preparing food and eating together may simply come from taking the time to complete each of those steps. For instance, deciding what to plant and grow, preparing the soil, mulching, watering and eventually harvesting herbs, vegetables and fruits of that collective labor means that teammates have spent significant time together on a shared enterprise. Stephen Ritz of the

Bronx Green Machine has found ways to accelerate this experience with vertical gardens within classrooms that might be adopted by teams of adults. The deepening connection between teammates emerges from conversations about their own experiences with gardening in the past– hours spent with friends and family, varying levels of expertise, and the development of patience as the plants grow, wither, recover, and are eventually enjoyed.

Preparing the food (grown together, brought from home or purchased in the local market) extends the connection of the team to another realm; sharing the origins of favorite recipes that connect you to friends and family, learning about food from different cultures around the world, learning about preferences and allergies and the relationship to food. Depending upon the resources and time available, teams can experiment with cooking in each person's home, utilizing culinary spaces in a school or signing up for cooking classes.

Eating the food together adds another dimension to becoming actively connected. Eating the food can include traditions for setting the table, types of place settings, working from a buffet, or serving each other family-style.

2) Dancing, Singing, Making Music

As a team becomes more comfortable with each other, dancing and music may become incorporated into the team-building process. Just as teammates have varying levels of experience and confidence in growing, harvesting, preparing and eating food, the physical activity of dancing, singing and making music is likely to be met with varying levels of enthusiasm.

Have you ever tried performing a ceremonial Maori dance called a haka? The act of dancing may bring out musical preferences, childhood stories of dance lessons, school dances, cultural traditions and much more. Adding dance to your team toolkit can be rewarding, with the understanding that dance can also make some people uncomfortable with their ability to follow a routine or beat, and thus excluded from the cohesion of the team.

Just as there is power in the stories that flow through our bodies and become part of a collective story, the physical act of singing and making music releases endorphins (Launay & Pearce, 2020) and oxytocin in the brain (Hamelink, 2020), stimulating social bonding.

3) Adventuring

Adventuring as a team covers a wide territory based on the location, abilities, and passions of the team. In one community, team sports such as pickleball, tennis, volleyball, basketball, baseball, or soccer might be the default team practice. In other communities, rock climbing, zip lines, rafting, hiking, and camping might be the most accessible team experience. Encourage your team to play table tennis, take a hike, go camping, cycling, etc. The less purposeful and less competitive, the better. Team adventures can also be created within a building such as leading (from behind) blind-folded teammates through a maze of desks in the hallway or solving challenges in an escape room, which could even be designed by young people.

In our conversations with organizations such as Outward Bound, the Bozeman Field School, and One Stone, educators, and young people report that combining the team adventure with an extended disconnection from digital technology deepens the connection of teammates.

Teams benefit from creating a culture of connection through stories, food, and physical activity. It is our experience that, when teammates have numerous points of connection, facing challenges together becomes easier. The team has gotten to know each other in the fullness and complexity of their lives and is able to understand their collective sources of strength or potential barriers to flowing with challenges.

4.2. Strategies for Flowing with Challenges

The elephant in the room, unspoken truths, hidden assumptions, unconscious bias. Our language is rich with naming the unnamed sources of conflict. Let's be honest with ourselves: we have all had to deal with problems, conflicts, or rather, challenges when working within a team.

Our aspiration in this section is, first, to raise **awareness** of the sources of misunderstanding, miscommunication, tension and conflict when interacting and being a member of a team; second, to **acknowledge** that those **uncomfortable situations** are part of the interaction process and a learning opportunity; and third, to share **strategies** for facing challenges as a team. We will begin with identifying the assumptions we might make that can undermine the cohesion of a team, but first, some wisdom from young people, was captured in our conversation with Suzie Boss.

4.2.1 Awareness

Our awareness begins with examining the assumptions we make based on our life experiences and biases that may lead us to misunderstand the potential contributions of our teammates. We might make assumptions about the capabilities of our peers due to their age, gender, culture/race, or level of education. We might misunderstand a comment from a peer based on those assumptions. Our experience with team members might impact our current teamwork. For example, we remember our new colleague as a former student and may have difficulty embracing them as a peer. Or we may feel more comfortable forming a team with people we are more aligned with.

Wilck and Lynch (2018) suggest that the first question we need to ask ourselves is WHY? What are the reasons that our team is not working well together? What type of elephant is hidden in the team's room? How many elephants are we not able or willing to acknowledge? How are those elements (and elephants) impacting our work as a team?

Let's be mindful and raise awareness on a key issue: diverse teams may solve complex problems better than homogeneous ones. As Rock, Grant, and Grey (2016) affirm, diversity can affect us all differently with problematic interpretations mixed with deeply rooted values; but still, if we promote diverse teams they will outperform homogenous teams even if homogenous teams feel more effective. Why so? Because precisely because it's harder. While on a homogenous team, people readily understand each other and collaboration flows smoothly, giving the sensation of progress; dealing with outsiders causes friction, which feels counterproductive. "Similarly, confronting opinions you disagree with might not seem like the quickest path to getting things done, but working in groups can be like studying (or exercising): no pain, no gain." (2016, para. 8)

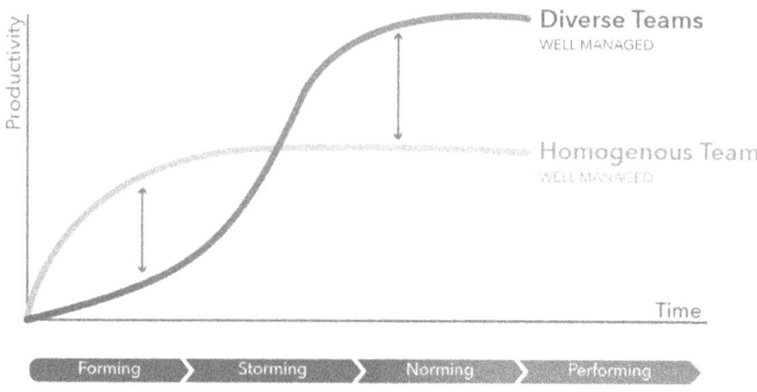

Figure 4.1 Based on Korn Ferry

Other Voices

"Trust lies at the heart of a functioning, cohesive team. Without it, teamwork is all but impossible." (Lencioni, 2002, p. 195)

Bias

Bias, a systematic error in judgment, may interfere with the ability to be impartial in any social relationship. Therefore, raising awareness of its presence in multiple forms may help us to be alert to the way it influences our thoughts and behaviors when interacting with our teammates. Our bias is shaped by our experiences, values, personalities, preferences, and perspectives.

To harness the power of diverse groups to cultivate spaces of mutual empowerment, confidence, agency, and engagement in building the collective wisdom of any group, we must first create those diverse teams and encourage individuals to become consciously aware of biases. Next, we need to work with the biases we hold as individuals and as a collective whole, ultimately developing a collective consciousness to better meet our mutual purpose.

Knowing myself, and what I bring to a group, allows me to identify more quickly the commonalities I share with members of a team and the differences that exist. It also allows me to identify where I might hold biases, understandings, and ways of doing that could disrupt the cultivation of an effective team and the collaborative process.

A focus on bias–specifically implicit bias–is foundational to increasing the effectiveness of teaming strategies. We do this because implicit bias creates attitudes (positive or negative) that affect our understanding, actions, and decisions in an unconscious manner. It impacts our thoughts and actions that discriminate or disproportionately favor one person or group of people over another based on their identities, characteristics, beliefs, ways of knowing and doing, or our perceptions of the person or group. It impacts assumptions we make about someone's abilities and potential which can have positive and negative impacts on the collective whole. What we also know is that implicit bias is developed over a lifetime. It is pervasive and everyone possesses it. The good news is it is changeable!

Your ability to change the biases you hold depends on your ability to know yourself in an honest and open manner. Being able to name your bias and create actionable steps or strategies to better identify when it exists can avoid undesirable and destructive decision-making based on these biases. However, recognizing when you are making a biased decision is arguably the most difficult part of this process.

Over time, identifying and addressing your bias will become easier. Once you recognize it and implement appropriate strategies you can better address how your bias might impact your decision-making and behaviors. Ideally, this will create more productive and inclusive teaming experiences.

Erin implemented a 7-step design process (see Team Challenge: Unraveling Bias below) weaving one of the Design Thinking strategies we explore in Chapter 5 with a culminating study of research, frameworks, and practices that address bias.

Team Challenge: Unraveling Bias
This 7-step design process develops ways of thinking that can help support and guide you through the work of unraveling bias in an equitable, just, and personalized way. The framework creates an interactive process for you to address bias, as an individual and collective group.

*1. **Understand** bias (empathize)*
This step provides individuals the space to build empathy, begin to shift and change perspectives and see through different lenses with ways of thinking. Questions an individual or team might ask include:
- *What is bias?*
- *Why does understanding bias matter?*
- *How does it impact individuals? This includes myself and those around me.*
- *How does it impact me being an effective teammate?*
This step evolves as you do this work -it might start with simply understanding that bias exists and evolves through your work and reflective process.
The strategy of categorization that gives rise to unconscious bias is a normal aspect of human cognition. Understanding this important concept can help individuals approach their own biases in a more informed and open way (Burgess, 2007).
*2. **Recognize** (accept) that you hold biases.*
Working with immediate impressions from images -addressing quick judgements that we learn to make overtime from our experiences and exposures. Holding space to recognize where my bias exists.
*3. **Identify** (define) what your biases are.*
You can take assessments and conduct reflection activities to identify these biases. You can start with Harvard's Implicit Association Test (IAT) to begin this initial assessment.
*4. **Examine** (ideate) your own biases and their effects on yourself and others. This will provide you with a better understanding*

about yourself and reasons why you hold these biases and why they are important to address. It will also help you to remove blinders that might exist to better understand how these strategies might impact you.

*5. **Develop** (prototype) strategies to plan for addressing your own biases.*

These strategies will be purposeful and specific to your needs when considering how these biases might present themselves in actions and words.

*6. **Address** (test) these biases with your strategies when you recognize them.*

Put your planning into practice recognize biases and utilize your strategies.

For example, as a cis gender female, my pronouns are never misused. By stating my pronouns in my introduction, email signature, online bio, name online, etc. I am working to cultivate spaces where pronouns are used and respected. I am also preparing myself for dialogue with others who may disagree. This way, I am preparing myself for interactions that work towards safe and inclusive environments

*7. **Reflect** on the effectiveness of the strategy:*
- *How did it impact my perceptions?*
- *How did it impact others?*
- *Am I thinking and feeling differently?*
- *Do I have new understandings?*

*As a team, you can have discussions surrounding this work. These discussions can lead to identifying **Guiding Principles**. For example, "We aspire to be conscious of the bias we bring to our work together and actively seek to make decisions that are not influenced by that bias."*

The process described above can be linear but does not need to be. Each of the steps allows us to hold space for our biases and to recognize and acknowledge that holding space for our biases is hard work. It is also ongoing, never-ending, and lifelong. We believe that through this work we can cultivate environments of trust, communication, purpose, and where everyone feels a sense of belonging, and agency over their work, that they matter and make a difference on that team.

Exploration of implicit bias is not sufficient as a stand-alone exercise. It is also necessary to unpack your biases and underlying assumptions through self-reflection and discussion. Implicit biases can be positive or negative perceptions. Either way, they have an impact on how we work with and interact with others. A person tends to act on their biases under stress or in moments where split-second decisions must be made.

Implicit biases are not intentional. A person may hold biases that have not been acknowledged or explored. It is important for an individual to avoid getting defensive or assuming they do not have biases but acknowledge and address them. This can be difficult work for many reasons. It can be difficult to honestly acknowledge the biases held by an individual. It can be perceived as too uncomfortable to talk or think about biases. Often, individuals will ignore the biases that are clearly held and transferred into their actions and interactions with other people.

Recognition and acknowledgment can support a person's work to identify where their implicit biases impact their work with others and develop ways to hold themselves accountable to each other for positive growth as a team.

Have you ever considered measuring attitudes and beliefs that we may be unwilling or unable to report because of different possible reasons? Try taking the Implicit Association Test (IAT), "an effective educational tool for raising awareness about implicit bias" (Project Implicit, 2011, para. 3). If you are curious and eager to learn more about yourself, why not use it to reflect and get insights on how becoming aware of your own bias can benefit you to grow successfully when being part of any team?

4.2.2 Acknowledge Uncomfortable Situations

When people with different perspectives are brought together, there is a natural or purposeful reaction to ignore or gloss over the differences that exist in the interest of group harmony. When, in fact, differences should actually be taken seriously and highlighted.
- David Rock, Heidi Grant Halvorson & Jacqui Grey (2016)

Embracing the diversity of the team can create a better understanding of the individuals in the group, what they value, how they operate, and how they might align or differ from each other. It can also allow for the recognition of where the individual might bring insight, experience, or different perspectives that can be beneficial and valued.

There are many ways that teams can use different points of view to enhance the teaming experience. Members can be assigned distinct roles (Artistic, Event, and Finance Manager), thus increasing diversity of viewpoints. These teams tend to come up with better ideas than homogeneous teams – but only if they have been explicitly trying to take the perspectives of their teammates. This requires a team to work *with* the differences to benefit from them.

Teams can also highlight the value of multiculturalism and diversity within the identities and practices represented on the team. The powerful learning experience, name origin stories, and cultural iceberg exercises referenced in Team Challenge: One Day Workshop, each represent ways of deepening connections between teammates and discovering shared values. The practice of valuing these differing viewpoints can foster a culture where seeking out the benefits becomes the norm.

It is important to note that diversity is not always a panacea and it can, at times, produce corrosive conflict. When that happens, it is often because team members are bringing different values, rather than different ideas, to the table. Engaging in values exercises, like the ones detailed in Chapter 1 can help to reveal shared values early in the formation of a team.

For a team to benefit from the unique experiences and perspectives cultivated within a diverse team, team members must feel welcome and respected. Their perspectives and worldviews need to be heard, understood, and valued. This is important because these perspectives and worldviews impact the way they contribute to the group, interpret the work, and interact with the strategies being used and systems in place.

This work can create moments of unfamiliarity and discomfort. However, if teams can recognize and experience these moments as catalysts for creativity and deep thinking, the process will eventually be welcomed and celebrated. Teams may begin to actively seek out these uncomfortable situations knowing the benefits they create.

4.2.3 Ways to Flow with Challenges

Think of this section as a set of tools for preventing conflict as well as strategies to employ once conflict has emerged.

Making Mistakes and Intentionally Failing

We all make mistakes. Mistakes are a part of the learning process and help us to build neuroplasticity. We can learn from mistakes purposefully and increase our ability to collaborate as a result. Placing people in physically challenging situations- ropes course, for example- "experience what it feels like to depend on, and be supported by their colleagues" (Edmondson, 2012, p. 262).

Mistakes and failure are often viewed negatively and as something to be avoided. But what if we think of mistakes as learning opportunities or begin to use the acronym *FAIL: First Attempt In Learning* to reframe our relationship to failure? Making things (art, music, drama, video, food, textiles, science) to learn opens other opportunities to push solutions to the point of failure and develop an understanding of why that failure occurred before moving ahead. It can also be utilized to emphasize the importance of multiple drafts and revisions. Failure tests the cohesion, empathy, and communication skills of the team.

Team Challenge: Water Bottle Rocket Challenge
We could begin to intentionally design learning experiences to require failure as a part of the process. For example, many schools have water bottle rocket challenges using pre-made kits. What if the kits were expanded to include 5oo ml, 1 liter, and 2 liter bottles? Fins and cones of different materials and proportions? Parachutes of various dimensions?

Now add to the challenge: vary the volume of water within the bottle and vary the pressure applied. Now add a few more challenges: which team can use the least amount of material (by weight) to launch a rocket the greatest distance above the ground AND come closest to a target on the ground below.

This collection of challenges can only be achieved through many mistakes and failures. Once a team succeeds in using the least material and reaches the highest altitude and closest proximity to the target, they have an opportunity to try again- with less material, greater heights, and more precise approaches to landing.

Shifting Perspective Games

Perhaps take time to play the game OuiSi ("we-see" or Yes-Yes). It is an award-winning set of 210 Visual Connecting Photo Cards with activities and games that foster creativity, ignite curiosity, and most importantly, help each of us to see other perspectives and make connections we may not have previously considered.

Teach how to use an I-message

An I-message is a de-escalation strategy that supports self-expression and conflict resolution. The I-message focuses on stating something that may negatively impact us by avoiding attacking the other person or placing the blame on them; as it usually happens with a "You message".

Try replacing a "You-message" with an "I-message" and raise awareness on how you feel how the other reacts and how the situation evolves and solves.

You-message	I-message
You make me feel..., when you...	*I feel __ (say your feeling)* *when you __ (describe the action)* *because __ (say why the action connects to your feeling)* e.g. "I feel disappointed when you say you will do something because in the end, you don't commit to it, and I need that to continue making progress with my work."

Restorative Practice

Some of our mistakes impact our teammates more than others. It might be our words, our actions, or our beliefs about each other. It is necessary to have the willingness to repair any harm caused, even unintentionally, through mediation and restorative conferencing. For that purpose, we may want to get deeper into the *Restorative Justice philosophy*, which "has roots in Indigenous justice systems, based on the idea that the well-being of a community and its members are preserved through communication, emotional connection, understanding, and meaningful relationships." (Chicago Public Schools Restorative Practices, 2017, p. 2)

As teams form their agreements, a simple restorative practice might be included, such as the one noted below.

Conflict Model Instrument (Thomas-Kilmann)

The TKI assessment (2002) is used to help both individuals and teams navigate through conflict management, understanding each person's style and how those can make an impact on interpersonal and group dynamics. It supports:

- Team building—The TKI assessment's simple and effective conflict resolution model improves team functioning, helping members work together more effectively.
- Leadership development—The TKI assessment's insights enhance leaders' conflict management skills and ability to reconcile differences.
- Performance improvement—The TKI assessment helps eliminate barriers to success in the workplace.
- Stress reduction—The TKI assessment gives employees the capacity and tools to remove a common cause of work-related stress.
- Retention—With the means to address conflict effectively, employee morale and success improve, enabling you to build a stronger organization and retain the best talent.

The TKI assessment is easy to use and doesn't require certification. It can be administered alongside the MBTI® assessment for deeper insights into personality and conflict management.

Completing the Stress Cycle

Teammates might feel a bit raw if conversations have revealed the sources of assumptions and biases of peers. It may be helpful to return to the listening practices described earlier in this chapter and to acknowledge the sources of stress in the relationships of the team.

Although Emily and Amelia Nagoski (2019) focus on the value of completing the stress cycle to avoid burnout in individuals, teams may benefit from utilizing these same practices. Each of the elements can be used to complete the stress cycle involving a shift of focus from intellectual practices to physical practices such as movement, creating, hugging, laughing, breathing, and crying. Humor is one of the 16 habits of mind (finding humor) that may be employed to break the tension in the stress cycle, using the improvisation strategies noted earlier in this chapter.

Resilient Teams

Derek Peterson developed the Web of Support framework to help develop resilient behaviors in young people, but his work is relevant to the creation of resilient teams of any age. The Web of Support builds resilience through awareness of adult anchors, who in turn are anchored by their own anchors. The web of tangible support and intangible values weaves a launch pad, filter, and safety net for each young person, or in the case of a team, each teammate. This web provides a safe place for experimentation, and opportunities to push oneself, or our entire team beyond our comfort zone, knowing our anchors will be there as we fail, recover, and persist.

4.3 Strategies for Decision-Making

If educators have spent their careers working alone, there has been
no need for a team much less making decisions as a team. Even those
educators or leaders who may have been working in teams for long
can find more practical and effective ways for decision-making, and
problem-solving. Moreover, successful decision-making tools help
empower introverts, break the pattern of the most vocal participant

taking charge, and ensure every member's voice and choice within their teams.

We have worked with schools and educational institutions that continue to have educators work alone but share these decision-making tools with learners. It is a bit like the proverbial letters to advice columnists asking for help "for a friend." Sometimes learners can build the path for future teams of educators to follow. And what if educators and school leaders walked the talk first? Remember that **modeling** is one of the eight forces that we must master to transform schools (Ritchhart, 2015).

We have many opportunities to make decisions, both good and bad, and become better at making decisions over time. If we make a good decision, everything seems to run smoothly. But if we make a bad decision, does it mean we are a bad person? Obviously not! We just made the least appropriate decision on that particular occasion.

As we noted in the discussion of celebrating milestones, successes, and failures, teams need this same foundation as well: if the decisions they make do not go well, it does not mean it is a bad team, but simply not the best decision for the team at that time. They, too, can fail, recover, persist, and become more resilient over time. In fact, "resilience is often identified as one of the factors that helps individuals get ahead. But few of us work entirely alone, and how our teams persevere matters just as much as how individually resilient we are" (Kirkman et al., 2019, p. 1).

Teams face different kinds of decision-making. The more strategies we have to make a decision, the better. We'll be able to apply one or another according to a particular situation, or the moment our team is in. The following strategies offer you some ideas on how to be more effective and thoughtful when making decisions, rather than defaulting to simple, majority rules. We suggest beginning with the SEEDS Model for addressing bias, to prepare the ground before starting any decision-making process.

SEEDS Model for Addressing Bias

The NeuroLeadership Institute developed the SEEDS model to "mitigate the biases that negatively affect decision-making." Utilizing the acronym SEEDS (Similarity, Expedience, Experience, Distance & Safety), each of these elements represents an opportunity to understand the sources of bias and adopt new behaviors to address them.

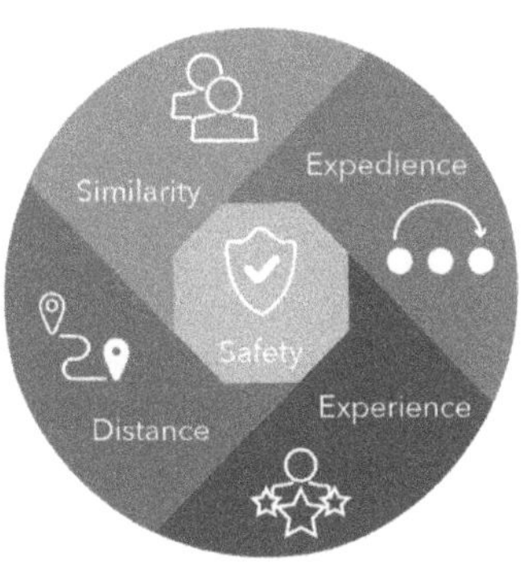

Similarity bias – *We prefer similarity over difference.*
Teams can overcome our similarity bias by forming relationships with people who see the world in ways that are different from our own.

Expedience bias – *We prefer to act quickly.*
Teams can develop multi-step processes that slow down our decision-making process while increasing information gathering.

Experience bias – *We take our own perception to be the objective truth.* Teams can create processes that invite others to share feedback and their perspective and discover additional paths forward.

Distance bias – *We prefer what's close over what's far away*
Teams can seek input from peers on other teams, other schools, in other communities before proceeding with their decision.

Safety bias – *We protect against loss more than we seek out gain.* Teams can address this bias by reducing the emotional immediacy of a decision and envisioning the impact of the desired future outcome.

The SEEDS model assists a team in developing a "common language around bias to help each other make smarter decisions."

What Works Framework

It is common to share information with a group and ask for feedback. Although we have used the three questions "What Works?" "What Could Be Better?" "What's Missing?" for more than a decade, we still have individuals jump in and say: "So you want us to list the Pros and Cons of each option, right?" Not exactly. The feedback that emerges from these three simple questions consistently results in a deeper understanding of the options you are considering and provides opportunities for improvement.

The items identified under "What Works?" represent an important foundation that many other items can be built upon. "What Could Be Better?" captures elements that need additional development. No idea is perfect. "What's Missing?" collects ideas that were not considered but should probably be explored as the work continues.

This framework can be learned by anyone from age 5 to 100. It applies to presentations, videos, writings, science experiments, musical performances, building and product designs, works of art, athletic performances, etc. It can be offered in the form of quick verbal feedback, summary notes, or visible notes on a wall chart or on a digital tool, like the 'What Went Well Retrospective' board. (EasyRetro, n.d.).

The "What Works Framework" is unlikely to result in making a decision, but it provides a helpful foundation for the more deliberate decision-making tools that follow. For example, a group of year 7 learners in Kempsey, NSW Australia had developed several options and were considering which option they would identify as their preferred alternative. After extensive discussion of each alternative, they could not decide. The words that came next were precious to those of us in attendance. "What if we built all three options first, and then decided?" They were identifying what worked, what could be better, and what was missing and agreed that more information (in the form of better prototypes) would be needed to complete their evaluation.

Once we have set the ground for analysis, we are in the position to discuss how to proceed with a decision-making strategy of our choice. Here we share three possible strategies to consider. Just choose the most suitable one according to your team, the type of decision, and the circumstances.

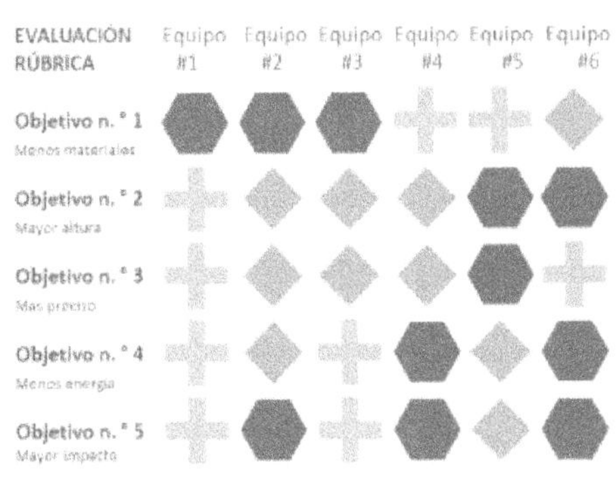

Guiding Principles

Another foundational exercise is to identify a series of guiding principles and to evaluate a range of options utilizing those guiding principles.

Teams of participants use a simple graphic response of Red (octagon), Yellow (diamond), and Green (plus) dots (like a traffic signal) indicating poor, adequate, and good fit with a guiding principle.

The guiding principles for a project might be:
   o   Uses the least material.
   o   Achieves highest altitude.
   o   Lands with the greatest precision.
   o   Uses the least energy.

This process can be used by one team examining many options or for multiple teams looking at each option individually. This exercise often reveals a preferred alternative through the graphic power of many green dots with a few yellow dots. What may appear to be a preferred alternative may have a single red dot which should be ignored at your peril. That red dot represents one team's assessment of a single guiding principle, but also a source of future resistance to funding the preferred alternative, or worse yet, a conflict once the preferred alternative has been implemented. It is best to engage the team that assigned a red dot to that guiding principle and determine if more time, more information, or new thinking is needed to address the concern.

Many ideas emerge from guiding principles developed by a group during earlier stages of exploration. For example, you may be considering how you spend time, integrate technology, and form relationships. In addition to the ideas your reporter captured in the form of notes and diagrams, and shared by your reporter, the reflector spent time carefully listening to the work of the group and attempted to express those insights in the form of a guiding principle.

Six Thinking Hats Method

This decision-making strategy has proved to be a time-saving method, and its most striking benefits are seen in group discussions or conversations. In those situations, the method provides a framework that is much more effective than argument or free discussion (De Bono, 1992) It removes personal egos by providing a neutral and objective exploration of a subject, allows one to focus on one thing at a time and the full picture emerges at the end. Every member, as a thinker, is looking in the same direction at the same time, so different points of view are shared alongside the others. This is why it is called parallel, or lateral, thinking. Consequently, it is about adding, not about counterarguing, making the fullest use of everyone's intelligence and experience (De Bono, 1992, p. 7).

These six different color hats correlate as follows:
- White: It is concerned with objective facts and figures (neutral and objective);
- Red: It gives an emotional view (emotions and feelings);
- Black: It points out the weaknesses in an idea (somber and serious, cautious and careful);

-   Yellow: It covers hope and positive thinking (sunny, positive and optimistic);
-   Green: It indicates creativity and new ideas (grass, vegetation, and abundant, fertile growth);
-   Blue: It is concerned with control, the organization of the thinking process and its steps, and the use of the other hats.

Figure 4.2 Six Thinking Hats based on DeBono

When everyone in the team knows about the color code and their functions, you are ready to sit at a discussion table and use one hat or another easily to make your decisions. To add a bit of fun, you might distribute the six hats around the table or around the circle and ask each teammate to view the challenge from that perspective. You could display the hats in your planning center or meeting room and changeup who wears them each time you come together.

Decision-Making Thinking Skill

From the Thinking-Based Learning (TBL) perspective, the decision-making thinking skill elaborates on the development of efficient and skillful thinking, which can be definitely put into practice to make effective and well-grounded decisions.

As a team, we can also develop better decision-making habits, so our decisions are not as hasty, narrow, scattered, and fuzzy, as they commonly are.

As it happens with every thinking skill, getting started takes time and requires following each step mindfully, especially with such a complex skill. The first step consists in co-creating a thinking map, an organized series of guiding questions:

- What makes this decision necessary? What is creating the need for a decision?
- What are the options? Are there unusual ones that we should consider in that particular circumstance?
- What consequences would result if we took these options? Are there long-term consequences, consequences for others, or consequences that we might not ordinarily consider?
- How likely are these consequences? Why? What evidence or reasoning is there for thinking that they are likely? Is this information reliable?
- Do these consequences count in favor of or against the options being considered?
- How important are these consequences- not just for us, but for those affected by them? Are there some consequences that are so important that they should count more than others?
- When we compare and contrast the options in the light of the consequences, which option is best?
- How can we carry out this decision? (Swartz & Parks, 1994).

The following image summarizes the process, and lists all the diverse skills which are into play:

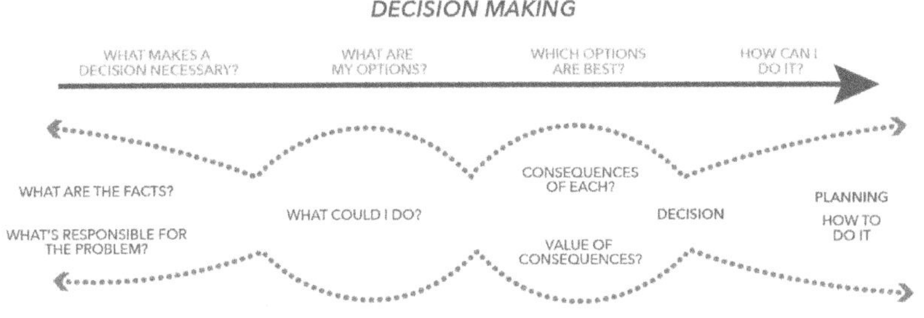

Figure 4.3: Decision Making based on Swartz & Parks (1994)

These questions can be also supplemented with graphic organizers to organize thinking and manage information in skillful decision-making (Swartz & Parks, 1994) as you can see in figures 4.4 and 4.5. Teams that need more structure will find these tools of value.

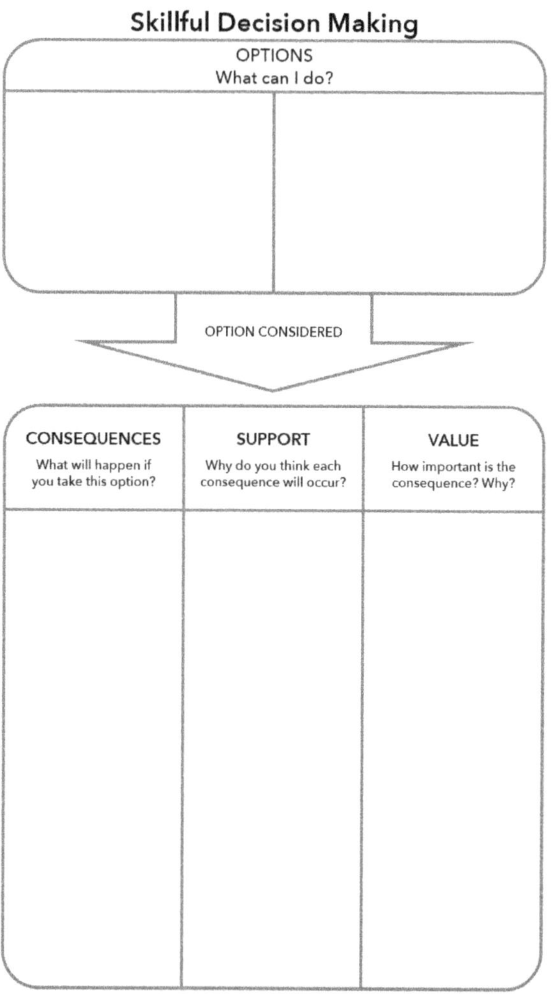

Figure 4.4 Skillful Decision Making based on Swartz & Parks (1994, 42-43)

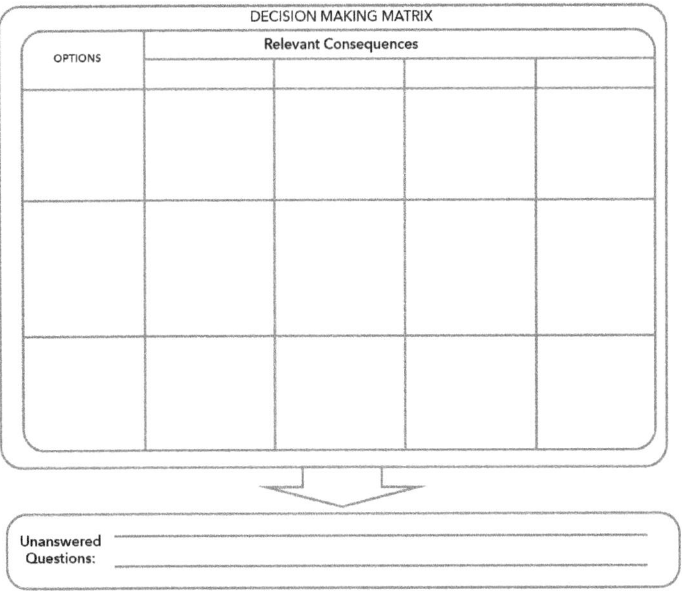

Figure 4.5 Decision-Making Matrix based on Swartz & Parks (1994, 42-43)

Apart from these methods and strategies, many other ways can give answers to decision-making, depending on the type of decision, how important it may be, and the circumstance. Each team will choose the most appropriate tools, combine them in new ways, discover something new, and make a decision based on that new insight.

Team Challenge: One Potato: Laughing While Making Decisions

Group decision-making can be serious business. The United Nations has wrestled with potential sanctions for decades while pain and suffering continue. The Parliament of the United Kingdom struggled for 3 years over the decision to join and then leave the European Union.

Small groups deciding which option to proceed with become paralyzed with fear. Analysis paralysis. One Potato offers an opportunity to lighten things up.

One great thing about this tool is that you can pull it out at any time: "Is it time to use One Potato?" or "Don't make me use One Potato to resolve this conflict!"

> *One potato, two potatoes, three potatoes, four.*
> *five potatoes, six potatoes, seven potatoes, more!*
> *(OUT- put one of your two fists behind your back)*

If you use this technique for making decisions, your team will develop its own norms such as, is it acceptable to change positions once the circle has been formed? (When some figure out the pattern and switch their advantage).

Not everything about forming a team is easy– growing as a team, facing challenges, and making decisions together. Each of those learning experiences contributes to your individual and collective growth. Ideally, telling stories, laughing, dancing, and making meals together are not one-time events, but become a visible part of the team culture you are creating. As team members change over time these events create opportunities to celebrate the contributions of teammates who are moving on, and to integrate new team members into the culture of the group. The reward is that you can accelerate your learning as you move from awareness to action.

After having read this chapter and having reflected on some essential issues, take your time to go back to your prior thoughts on going through it. Then, write about new ideas you may have learned, ideas that may have transformed your previous thoughts and beliefs, or why not extend them with new ideas you (and one of your teams) may have come up with after this reflective process.

Let's look at the practices highly effective teams engage in when their solid foundation of trust has been tested through growth, challenge, and collective decision-making. These are teams in action, and they are changing the world!

CHAPTER 5: TEAMS, LEARNING & METHODOLOGIES

Deeper learning for teams through Agile Learning, Design Thinking, Design For Change, eduScrum, Project Based Learning, Do It With Others, and Thinking Based Learning

"Teamwork is the secret that makes common people achieve uncommon results."

– Ifeanyi Enoch Onuoha , Author. Aba, Abia State, Nigeria

Teamwork may be key to enhancing methodologies like agile learning, project-based learning (PBL), thinking-based learning (TBL), and many others, by expanding practices of deeper learning moving from individual to collective intelligence.

Have you ever thought about how the power of teams can make an impact on our learners by applying one pedagogical practice or another, one methodological approach or another? Or how have your pedagogical practices been **enhanced** by teams? What about how your pedagogical practices have **impacted** teamwork or helped you to develop teams? And finally, how has learning been enhanced by using those pedagogical practices where teams were involved, in comparison to those where individuals were involved?

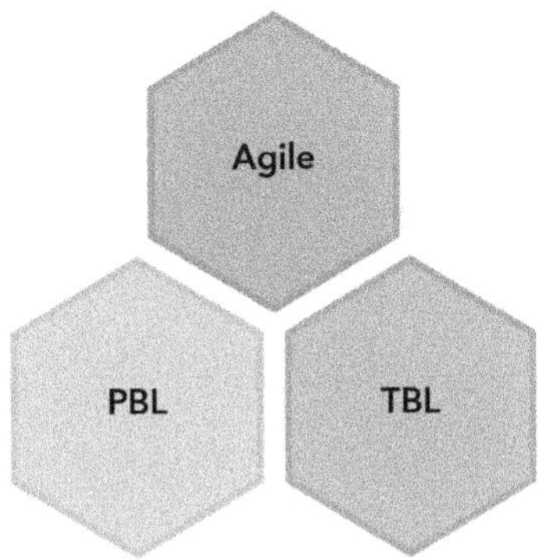

This chapter explores several methodological practices that enhance active and deep learning as they boost teamwork in multiple ways. You may think about many others, so feel free to add them to this list. We are aware of the many options we could have included here, like gamification, challenge-based learning, phenomenon-based learning, etc. However, we wanted to keep it as short and simple as possible and offer the opportunity for you to think about how other methodologies you are aware of connect with teams. This is why here we focus on three from diverse perspectives. Although we are analyzing them here separately one by one, they can be used interconnectedly and can enrich educational practices by complementing each other. Besides, they are listed in alphabetical order, with no interest in highlighting one over another. In the end, each methodology needs to serve a learning purpose for each specific educational context.

Before learning more about them give yourself, and your team(s), time and space to reflect upon your current practices and their connection with teams and teamwork.

__Your Turn:__ Take a moment to think about your current and past methodological practices, and what their connection with teamwork or collaboration has been like.

Your Turn: Which ones would you consider to nourish all the potential of a team? How do they manage to do that? Take your notes in the first section here:

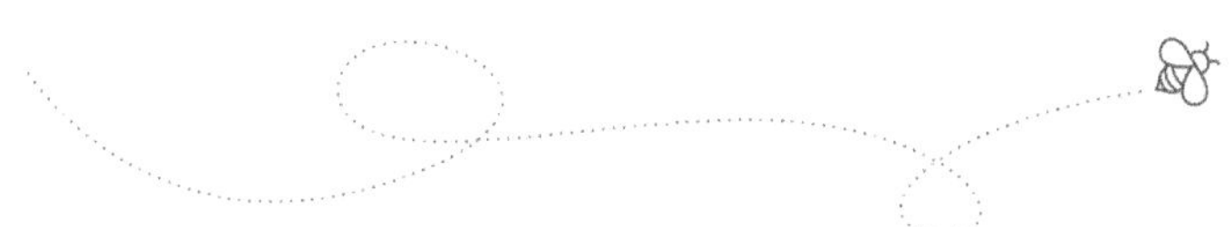

Your Turn: I used to think… // Write down all the ways you collaborate, or promote collaboration in your educational environments

Your Turn: Please share your prior experience, thoughts, or knowledge of Agile Learning, PBL, and/or TBL:

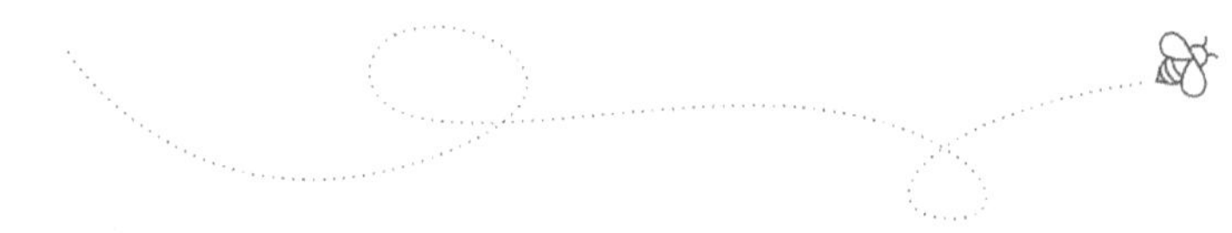

Your Turn: How have your pedagogical practices been enhanced by teams? What about how your practices have impacted teamwork or helped you to develop teams?

"Agile is a mindset, not a process or methodology."
– Dr. Ahmed Sidky- Agilist. Los Angeles, California, USA.

Although we are focusing on pedagogical practices, we find it is important to also consider how we approach the practices that we use. In order to successfully use agile learning practices you must cultivate an agile mindset. A mindset that allows a person and team to react quickly and adapt to changing circumstances and situations.

Therefore, before digging into agile learning, let's consider different types of mindsets that can help us approach these types of practices. Delving into mindsets can also be a good start towards achieving more successful teams. We have witnessed that employing a growth mindset, a benefit mindset, and an agile mindset will lead us to more effective teamwork.

A **growth mindset** implies cultivating a type of mindset that is open to growth and development in skills that we may not yet have achieved at a specific time in our lives (Dweck, 2014). It is also related to an openness to making mistakes and valuing the opportunities to learn from them. It contrasts with a fixed mindset, which considers potential as determined by birth. These traits are considered to be inherently stable and unchangeable over time.

Inspiring Video

Watch 'The power of believing that you can improve', TED Talk by Carol Dweck (17 December 2014).

As you can tell, employing a growth mindset can contribute to more successful teams formed by members who are eager to learn from one another.

A **benefit mindset,** coined by Ash Buchanan and Robert Ward (2020), "builds on a growth mindset, when we understand that our abilities can be developed – and we also understand we can transform towards a more caring and inclusive perspective" (p. 4). In successful teams, team members are aware of the potential development each other member has. They can also show more inclusiveness and be more empathetic as well as willing to care for each other.

Inspiring Video:

Watch 'Benefit Mindset in the Classroom', with Robert Ward (10 June 2019).

Finally, an **agile mindset** is grounded in a culture of learning. According to Ahmed Sidky, it allows "the learning to happen and then to be able to incorporate that learning back into the system". It embraces a very humane approach since one of its 12 principles focuses on human-centric and self-organizing teams. This approach embodies respect, collaboration, improvement, learning cycles, ownership, focus on delivering value, and the ability to adapt to change.

Inspiring Video:

Watch 'What is the Agile Mindset?, by Ahmed Sidky (16 Apr 2021).

Although the origins of agile are connected to software development, it has spread widely into the educational field mainly to boost successful teamwork. Even more, an Agile Schools

Manifesto has been developed as an adaptation of the original Agile Manifesto that teachers and school leaders can follow to improve educational success. Peha (2011) indicates the following four core values:

- Individuals and interactions over processes and tools,
- Meaningful learning over the measurement of learning,
- Stakeholder collaboration over complex negotiation, and
- Responding to change over following a plan.

Imagine the benefit for successful teams to not only focus on collaborative teamwork but also on the development of each person on the team. Employing these mindsets can give higher autonomy, voice, and choice, and promote small self-organized teams that belong to an interactive network of teams.

An agile mindset can relate to methodologies, like Design Thinking (Tim Brown) and SCRUM (Jeff Sutherland & Ken Schwaber), as well as to other approaches that have been specifically developed into the educational field such as Design for Change, *eduScrum* and the Designed InGenuity (DIG) Learning Framework.

You can get deeper insights by reading the following examples of methodologies based on an agile learning type. These include, among others:

- Design Thinking
- Design for Change
- eduScrum

Design Thinking

In this VUCAH (Volatile, Uncertain, Complex, Ambiguous, Hyperconnected) world there's a need to shift the way we understand education, moving from *what* students should learn and more on *how* they might learn. Design Thinking (DT) is a human-centered approach that learners can use to think creatively, plan, and take action to approach any kind of problem becoming change agents for both their community and the world (Lee, 2018). DT is about "believing we can make a difference, and having an intentional process in order to get to new, relevant solutions that create positive impact" (IDEO, 2012, p. 11). Therefore, it focuses on the 'how and why' rather than on the 'what', which educators can align with their state, regional or national curriculums.

The DT process consists of 5 phases, each of them with a particular goal, often illustrating the divergent and convergent aspects of DT in a linear form. Our revision of this diagram is organized in a circle, spiral, or web while retaining the important moments of divergence and convergence. The circular, spiral, or web-like diagrams open another door for promoting teamwork when we engage the whole team, rather than the experiences and thinking process of a single individual.

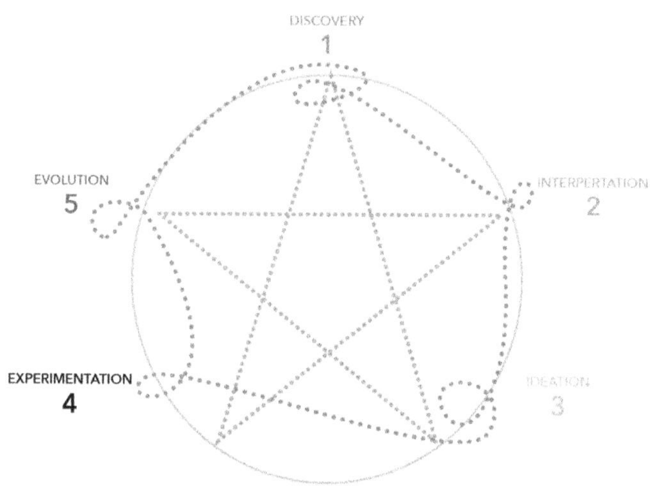

Figure 5.1 Cyclical version of the Design Thinking model based upon IDEO (2012)

Additionally, collaboration is thought to be inherent to DT, because solving complex challenges requires a team of persons with diverse talents, strengths, and perspectives. As teams may flow in multiple directions, these are some tips that IDEO recommends to build a successful team:

Start small. Start with a core group of 2 to 5 individuals. **Invite variety.** Choose team members who can bring different angles. **Assign roles.** Make sure everybody has a clear understanding of what to do. Distribute roles as the leader, the enthusiast, the coordinator, the nagger, etc. **Allow for alone time.** Individual work time must be assigned, though most of the work is done by the whole team.

Design for Change

As a simplified version of Design Thinking, Design for Change was developed for young people with a deeper purpose of making a difference in the world. This approach is based on a simple four-step design thinking process, Feel - Imagine - Do – Share (FIDS) (Goldman & Kabayadondo, 2016).

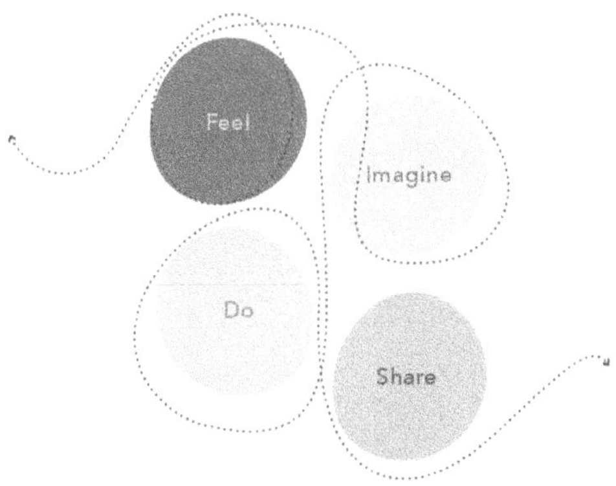

Figure 5.2 Circular version of FIDS Process based upon Sprintbase

As flexible as its methodology, this diagram can also be organized as a circle, spiral or web, so that "Share" is adjacent to "Feel" and the inspiration of the next phase of the process begins again.

The Design For Change FIDS model cultivates the 'I can' mindset through experiential learning. Unlike conventional approaches, it aims at offering both voice and choice to learners, and at empowering them by turning the 'I can't' mentality into an 'I CAN' one, as they work in teams to create change in their communities.

The impact of the FIDS process has been backed by research, such as the one conducted by *The Good Work Project,* which reaffirmed the impact of the FIDS approach on the development of skills like collaboration, creative thinking and empathy, as shown in the following graph.

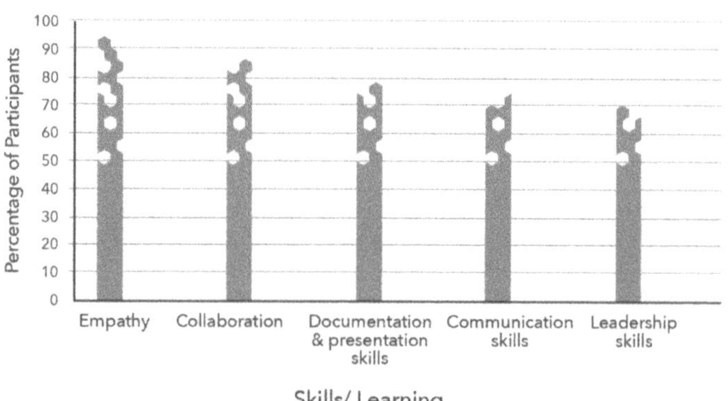

Figure 5.3 DFC Impact based on "The Good Project" research -Project Zero

The keys to developing projects using the DFC approach include agency, trust, empathy, collaboration, and listening:

Agency. Students are responsible for their projects whereas teachers become facilitators by assisting and guiding students throughout the whole process.
Trust. This is not a straightforward problem-solution approach, but a process where both divergent and convergent stages happen. Multiple solutions can be at play, and uncertainty is crucial. Have confidence in the process.
Empathy. Learning to see things in multiple perspectives is essential. Students nurture their comprehension and imagine possible solutions based on empathy.
Collaboration. "Working as a team is exciting and enriching: any team is stronger than any single person in it." Working in teams of 4-6 students can help classroom and project management too.
Listening. Encourage students to listen attentively to others, consider each other's opinions and ideas even when disagreeing. "What is important is not necessarily that their ideas be carried out but that the group reaches a common understanding of what has to be done" (Design For Change, 2016, pp. 10-11).

Thanks to DFC, young learners are able to develop specific skills that are essential for collaborative work, and most importantly, they put them into play in meaningful contexts for the benefit of a community. Learning makes real sense to learners as they become powerful changemakers in the present while developing projects in teams.

eduScrum ®

"eduScrum can give you wings!
But when you don't explain the WHY
you can't fly."

–Willy Wijnands, Founder of eduScrum
Alphen aan den Rijn, Netherlands

To understand eduScrum better, let's have a general overview of its origins, Scrum (2020): "a lightweight framework that helps people, teams and organizations generate value through adaptive solutions for complex problems" (Schwaber & Sutherland, 2020, p. 3). This particular framework is based on five living values: commitment, focus, openness, respect, and courage.

In Scrum (2020), "[t]eams are what get things done in the world of work. There are teams that make cars, answer phones, do surgery, program computers, put the news on [...] Certainly, there are artisans or artists who do work by themselves, but teams are what make the world go 'round. And they're what Scrum is based on" (Schwaber & Sutherland, 2020, p. 41).

With this first glimpse, it may be easier to understand how eduScrum was born from agile Scrum practices being applied in the classrooms of a Dutch chemistry teacher, Willy Wijnands. It is "a framework within which teachers and pupils tackle complex, challenging problems and pursue learning goals of the highest possible value in a productive and creative manner" (eduScrum, 2020, p. 6).

This framework implies a co-creative and (pro)active process that equips students to make a positive impact on the world together with others. Learners get the best out of themselves and their teams as they are made responsible for and given ownership over their own learning process. It aims at nourishing agile and self-organized life-learners by creating self-led and self-managed student teams who get involved in projects. It not only provides tools for creating projects but also for increasing personal growth, improving results, and learning how to work as a team.

Inspiring Podcast
Listen to this podcast 'How to Deploy Agile in Education and Create Self-Lead Student Teams with Willy Wijnands', by Enterprise Excellence Podcast with Brad Jeavons (23 November 2020)

"With eduScrum, cooperating teams will function optimally." (The Why of eduScrum, n.d.). These teams are self-organizing, co-responsible, and multidisciplinary, so they combine a wide range of skills and personal development areas. These self-organized teams are constituted by a product owner, an eduScrum Master (or team captain), and the team members. In a class, you see small teams of 4-5 learners working on their own, with their visual scrum board hung on the wall so it is visible at all times during the project. First, you see them co-creating their tree of great team values, their work agreements (Definition of Doing & Definition of Fun), and their Celebration Criteria. At some point, they may be holding a short meeting while standing, hanging up post-its on their kanban board, or reflecting on their work in a spring loop... This is what the whole process looks like:

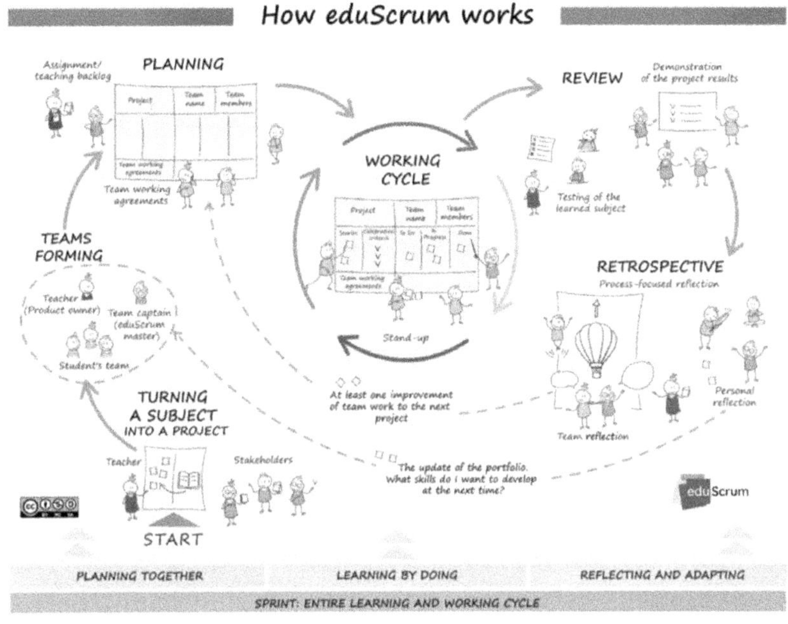

Figure 5.4 Retrieved from 'How' https://eduscrum.org/how-eduscrum-works/#how
Used by permission of Ekaterina Bredikina

eduScrum® also ensures that young people experience positive personal development. In their co-creative and (pro) active team, they are valued for their qualities, and they experience a sense of belonging and need. This strengthens their confidence in each other and themselves in a healthy way. Along the process, they develop a positive, future-oriented mindset, since eduScrum is based on endless possibilities for improvement.

Self-confidence, team skills, and a positive mindset are more important than ever for today's young people. In a rapidly aging society, much is expected of them. They are faced with crises on all fronts worldwide. eduScrum encourages them to develop into complete people who can be a meaningful part of and for their team.

5.2 Project-Based Learning

Project Based Learning (PBL or ABP, *Aprendizaje Basado en Proyectos* in the Spanish-speaking world), is a widespread pedagogical method that has its origins in schools at least back to 1918 when William H. Kilpatrick wrote about The Project Method. He emphasized the need for a wholehearted purposeful activity in a social situation for learning to happen.

Over the last century, PBL has been understood and practiced in slightly different ways, as we can tell from the many diverse practices and examples we can find all over the world. Here we focus on the approach shared by PBLWorks, who use the metaphor of PBL as the main course in a meal, rather than just a dessert (Larmer & Mergendoller, 2010). It is a teaching method in which students learn and gain both knowledge and skills by actively engaging in real-world and personally meaningful projects, as well as by investigating and responding to an authentic, engaging, and complex question, problem, or challenge for an extended period of time (PBL:Works, n.d.).

PBLWorks has developed a comprehensive, research-informed model to help any educator to develop a Gold Standard PBL experience. It comprises seven essential project design elements, as you can see in the following image. We have added some lines/text to clarify each element:

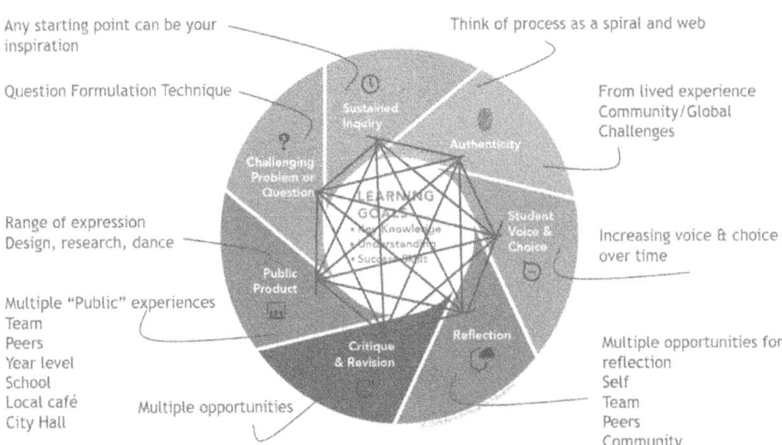

Figure 5.5 Multiple Entry Points for PBL Based on PBLWorks Gold Standard PBL

The power of PBL to promote learning multiplies when it is done in teams (Dumont et al., 2010).

> *The emphasis on teams in PBL is intentional, as they harness the social power of learning. It's not teamwork for the sake of teamwork, however. Collaboration is part of the authenticity of PBL, reflecting how problem solving unfolds in fields as diverse as health care, engineering, publishing, and the nonprofit sector. As complexity increases, collaboration among specialists becomes increasingly important.*
>
> *–Suzie Boss and John Larmer (2018, p. 82)*

Resources like the strategy guide 'Using Roles in Teams' and the collaborations rubrics help support the development of this soft (but powerful) skill, which becomes meaningful when working in teams within this approach (PBLWorks, 2020).

Project-Based Learning Resources

Numerous organizations have adopted an open-source approach to project-based learning, sharing projects, rubrics, and more. Organizations that have made significant impacts in the area of project-based learning include:

Edutopia
Hewlett Foundation for Deeper Learning
PBL Works

PBL Schools/Networks:
Brightworks
Expeditionary Learning
High Tech High
NewTech Network
NuVu Studio

We are frequently asked to help tune PBL experiences to improve the connection of educators, and engagement of teams of learners. Three of the twenty, or more, tuning protocols we have developed that continue to improve team engagement include:

Question Formulation Technique

Rather than launching a project with a driving question or essential question, consider developing a short, simple, provocative statement using the 'Question Formulation Technique' (QFT) from *The Right Question Institute*. The provocative statement is used by learners to generate, modify, prioritize and pursue questions of their own. The questions generated help to establish the need for background knowledge, or for deeper dives into the emerging theme. The QFT can be used to re-group young people into teams with similar interests, rather than friendship groups.

Roles and Rotations

Initially assign roles (e.g. director, writer, actor, videographer, timer, etc.) to clarify contributions made by each learner. As the project continues, randomly rotate roles so each participant develops new expertise and perspective. Consider rotating projects between teams so that struggling teams inherit a new point of departure and well-developed teams take on challenges of another perspective.

Build in Failure

Making things (like art, music, drama, video, food, textiles, science...) to learn opens other opportunities to push solutions to the point of failure and develop an understanding of why that failure occurred before moving ahead. It can also be used to emphasize the importance of multiple drafts and revisions. Failure tests the cohesion, empathy, and communication skills of the team. And it is definitely a meaningful element of the learning process.

PBL-Aligned Methods

Apart from the tuning protocols mentioned above, when we think of PBL, what other types of aligned methods come to your mind?

It may depend on where we place the focus and on the elements we emphasize. To name a few, we could relate PBL to challenge-based learning, problem-based learning, passion-based learning, Do-It-With-Others (DIWO), service learning, etc. All of them may follow the same or pretty similar steps, but they may differ on the purpose, the role of both the learner and educator, the starting point, the type of output, the audience to address, and the means to do it.

Consider starting by looking inside us… What if we started with our individual passions, letting our intrinsic motivation play its role?

Passion-based learning

Passion-based learning is born from each learner's inner passions, and from our own passions indeed! By offering opportunities for learners to explore existing interests and passions, and discover new ones (both widely and deeply), we may be igniting a world of possibilities to end up connecting with their ikigai, their purpose in life. As Ainissa Ramirez (2013) puts it, "everyone is a geek for something; everyone has passion for something" (para. 10) Explore your passions. Connect with one of them. Share it. Model how that passion drives learning and makes it flourish. And you'll see it's contagious!

Problem-based learning

According to Savery (2006) problem-based learning is another learner-centered approach that empowers learners to conduct research, integrate theory and practice, and apply skills and knowledge from a wide range of disciplines or subjects to come up with a solution to a defined problem. This problem must be ill-structured and allow for free inquiry, as well as it requires teamwork and learner collaboration. Each learner becomes responsible for searching for relevant information which will be shared with the rest of their team so together they can make progress in the development of a viable solution for a real world type of problem. Although it was born in the health sciences, it has been extended to many other fields (Savery, 2006)

Challenge-based learning

Similar to PBL but may be considered a broader approach where challenges or quests are introduced to focus the intention of the learning. It is "collaborative and hands-on, asking students to work with other students, their teachers, and experts in their communities and around the world to develop deeper knowledge of the subjects students are studying, accept and solve challenges, take action, share their experience, and enter into a global discussion about important issues" (Apple, 2008, p.1). As practical examples, think of hackathons or edhacks (educational hackathons), where communities of different kinds are involved.

DIWO (Do-It-With-Others)

DIWO extends the DIY philosophy and PBL methodology to embrace collaborative efforts to take on challenges and reach a solution that comes in the form of creative media production. The DIWO approach may be found in peer programming, fab labs, digital manufacturing laboratories, maker spaces, maker cultures, and spaces of collaborative innovation such as community hackathons.

Doing anything with others to increase the power of 'I' creates an immediate need to form a team, whether that is a peer recruited to work on a coding challenge, creating a small team to fabricate prototypes, or a spontaneous hackathon team assembled on a Friday evening focused on presenting solutions to the community on a Sunday afternoon. Doing things and collaborating with others will lead you to do bigger things in life. Yet, ultimately, doing it for others may lead you even further: to a state of self-actualization by fulfilling one of the most significant needs Maslow (1943) proposed in his stages of human needs.

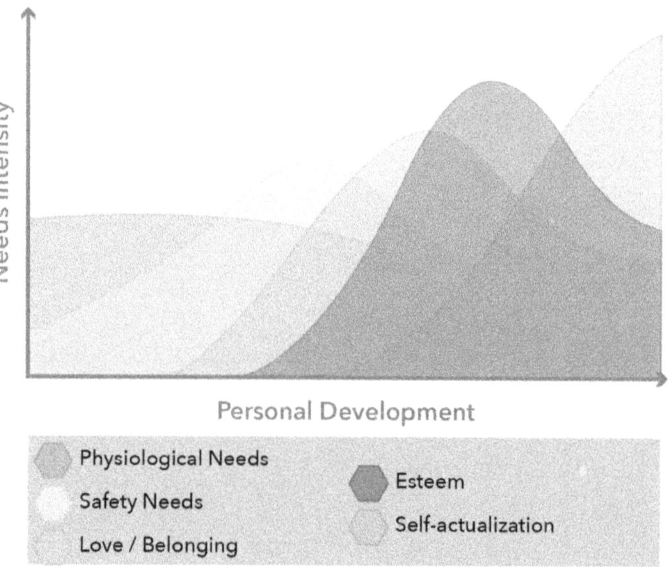

Figure 5.6 Maslow stages of human development based on Guttmann

Service Learning

Ultimately, service learning can be a great methodology to put into practice, since it has a clear goal to solve a real problem by meeting a need that comes from the learners' community, either local or global; and which requires teamwork to fulfill it. Even more, what if service was about connecting our passions to a community's needs?

Inspiring Video

Parker, J. (2015, June 3). *Service is connecting your passion to someone else's need.* [Video]. TED Talks.

This book is an example of a transformational journey, as it started from one of Nick's passions, and moved from an individual endeavor to a collective one, by inviting both Erin and Mar to join in this venture. The book then became our shared passion and we all kept this common goal to put this book together for the benefit of others. Our individual interests were enhanced as we learned from each other, challenged each other, and encouraged each other at every step of the writing process. Eventually, this book turned out to be the final product of our collective 'Do It For Others' (DIFO) PBL project with the aim to support and guide especially the educators' community who are willing to embrace it wherever they are in the world.

5.3 Thinking-Based Learning

> Skillful thinking – as self-initiated, self-monitored, self-corrected (if necessary), and goal-directed thinking – is an absolute necessity for success in our lives, our professions, and our participation in a democratic society (Swartz et al., 2008, p. 3).

If we want teams to be successful, how might every member of the team be engaged in skillful thinking? There are many different types of thinking we can engage ourselves in: routine thinking, impulsive thinking, intuitive thinking, and skillful thinking. Imagine every member of a team putting into play this variety of thinking. What would it be like if these types of thinking arose at the core of a team? If all the thinking contemplated in a team was only routine, impulsive, or intuitive thinking? On the contrary, how effective and successful could a team be if their thinking was skillful and careful?

Having a closer look at Thinking Based Learning may shed some light on how teamwork can be enhanced. Let's also unveil how skillful thinking in general can benefit teams, and let's consider what it involves and its elements. Thinking-Based Learning "offers an insightful contemporary research-based and experience-based vision of what learning could be like and should be like and, in a large number of wonderful classrooms around the world, is like" (Swartz et al., 2008, p. x).

It comprises three essential components: thinking skills, habits of mind, and metacognition (Swartz et al., 2008, p. 1). Let's get deeper into each of them.

Thinking Skills

A thinking skill is a relatively focused way of organizing thinking (Perkins & Swartz, 1991, p. 59). Perkins and Swartz (1991) classify them into three main categories: creative thinking, critical thinking, and analytical thinking.

When we think of thinking skills we need to think how to guide the learners to ask and answer a series of prompting questions which guide the thinking and can be made visible in a **thinking strategy map**. Once this strategy map is traced, the learners can use **graphic organizers** to record their thinking and to make it visible. A thinking organizer is "a concrete, verbal, and/or graphic structure that guides thinking" (Perkins & Swartz, 1991, p. 55).

Infusing thinking skills within team processes, like problem-solving or decision-making, can improve both the results and the processes experienced. You can go back to chapter 4 and have a taste of it learning more about the decision-making thinking skill in action.

Habits of Mind (HOM)

A habit of mind is defined as a disposition or inclination "to behave automatically and consistently in certain broad and constructive ways while thinking" (Swartz et al., 2008: 15). The Institute for Habits of Mind identifies 16 habits of mind, as shown in the following chart:

Figure 5.7 'Habits of The Mind Chart' (Habits of Mind Institute) retrieved from habitsofmindinstitute.org/what-are-habits-of-mind/

By becoming aware of and developing HOM, any team can benefit. When employing them, we may become better problem-solvers by having a disposition toward behaving intelligently when confronted with problems. When humans experience dichotomies, are confused by dilemmas, or come face to face with uncertainties—our most effective actions require drawing forth certain patterns of intellectual behavior. When we draw upon these intellectual resources, the results that are produced are more powerful, of higher quality, and of greater significance than if we fail to employ those intellectual behaviors (Costa & Kallick, 2021, para. 2).

One of the key habits of mind, 'persisting', has been studied by Duckworth and others as 'grit', an essential skill for individuals and teams. As Angela Lee Duckworth stated, "Grit is not just having resilience in the face of failure, but also having deep commitments that you remain loyal to over many years" (Perkins-Gough & Duckworth, 2013, p. 16). Developing grit as a team is a strategy for moving towards long-term goals as a team.

You may want to try this yourself and see where you are and where you want to move forward, by self-evaluating your HOM using a rubric. Reflecting on how to do that and even journaling about it can improve your habits and empower your skills to become part of any team. Even more, why not try this with a team you belong to, and see how this can help you all to become a more successful team!

Metacognition, thinking about your thinking

Thanks to metacognition, "people become aware of their usual thinking practices and gain the perspective they need to fine-tune or even radically revise those practices" (Perkins & Swartz, 1990, p. 64). Metacognition is enhanced by "stimulating students to articulate and verbalize their own thinking and to discover other, often better, ways of doing it" (Swartz et al., 2008, p. 72).

The **ladder of metacognition** is organized in four stages from Tacit to Aware to Strategic to Reflective, with aspirations to cultivate top-rung metacognition in the form of reflection (Perkins & Swartz, 1990). Although described as a ladder, the conceptual diagram can also be presented as a cycle, as our reflections lead to new tacit understandings, new awarenesses, new strategic insights, and new reflections.

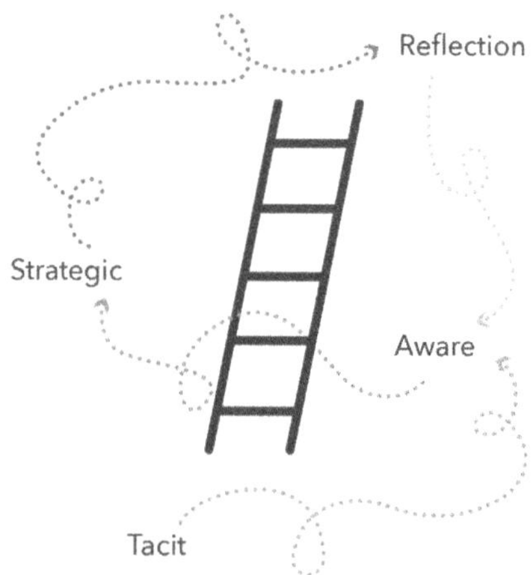

Figure 5.8 Ladder of metacognition based on Perkins & Swartz (1990)

When it comes to thinking about thinking and the skills that your team needs to develop as a whole, our four-part model of team formation may be helpful to provide time for thinking about the contributions your "Developing Insight" and "Sharing Wisdom" teammates are making to the growth of the team.

Practical Application

Nick worked with Kavita Tanna of Catalyst Learning Labs assisting a team of primary educators in New South Wales to develop a common design thinking process across the primary and secondary schools. The team had already worked with the 16 Habits of Mind framework, noted above, as well as the PBLWorks Gold Standard, Brightworks, Stanford d-school, 6 C's and were implementing an internal model of 4 E's (Explore, Express, Evaluate, Engage). The team aspired to create a simple process that every K-12 learner, educator, and community partner could utilize in their daily interactions.

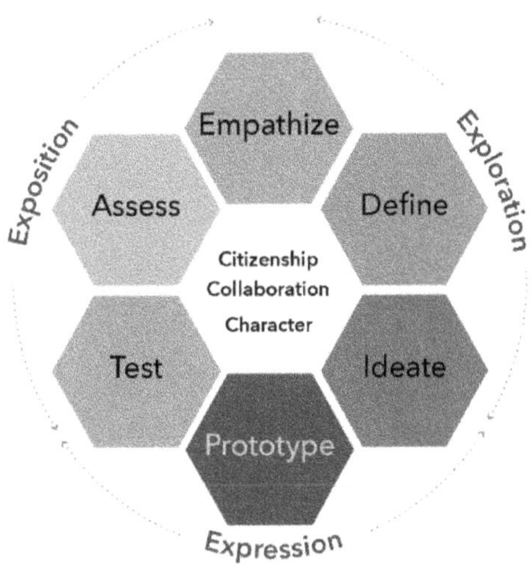

Figure 5.9 Cyclical Language Suites

This same diagram can also be expressed in a circle, spiral, or web bringing the assessment process in proximity to empathize, suggesting that the process begins again, and that any one of the 6 steps may be a point of entry to a project, drawing upon the strengths of each teammate.

Your Turn: *As you wrap up this chapter and add your insights here:*

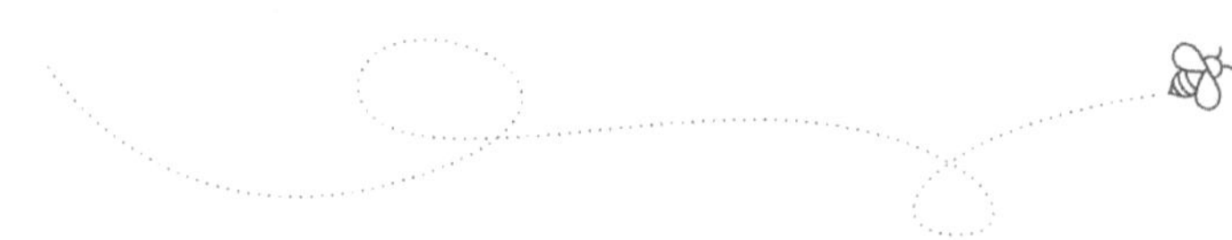

Your Turn: *Now I think…// What I think about these practices after having explored them*

Your Turn: So now I/we will…// How do your practices nourish the potential of the team? How has learning been enhanced by using those pedagogical practices where teams were involved, in comparison to those where individuals were involved?

Each of the practices discussed in this chapter is enhanced by teamwork. Agile practices rely heavily upon the strengths of each team member and their ability to contribute to a greater whole. The design thinking and design for change practices provide multiple entry points for teammates to stretch and share their strengths. eduScrum specifically creates roles for each teammate, and uses fast, iterative learning cycles to achieve growth in learning and growth in team practices. Project Based Learning is enhanced by working in teams with specific roles for each team member. Thinking Based Learning focuses the team on drawing upon the creative, critical and analytical skills of each teammate and then diving into each of the thinking skills, habits of mind and metacognitive processes both as individuals and as a team.

Each of these practices, and many others you may be aware of, can be combined in numerous ways, bringing greater depth to learning experiences and to the culture of the team. Activating a culture of teaming is an essential ingredient to our next chapter, Teams and Cultural Transformation.

CHAPTER 6: TEAMS & CULTURAL TRANSFORMATION
Supporting and Sustaining Transformation Through Teams

"A small group of thoughtful people could change the world. Indeed, it's the only thing that ever has"

- Margaret Mead – American Cultural Anthropologist

"Creating an Integrated Project Delivery contract and project is kind of like creating your own mini society. And within that society, and all the stress of learning, is a new way of working and collaborating. For some people, it's not easy. To collaborate that deeply, there are some people that by nature, can collaborate, but maybe not comfortably or physically in an open environment- introverts may want to spend time alone more often or take time to recharge away from a larger group. So you think of the stress of learning a new system, learning a new way to behave and participate."

- Darlene Cadman- WEFT Strategies. Scottsdale, Arizona. (2022)

Teams have the power to shape the culture of any organization. Culture includes the behaviors, language, artifacts, traditions, and stories of a family, organization, or community, and much more.

The transformation of a learning community requires an alignment of people, a shared vision, a common language, physical environments, and digital resources to interact. We have supported the transformation of communities through an exercise that draws upon the five elements of culture that many anthropologists seek to understand: behavior, artifacts, language, traditions, & folklore. It is our experience that transforming digital resources, technology, and physical environments impact the artifacts of a culture, whereas people are deeply embedded in the behaviors, language, traditions, and stories of a culture. Thus, we will begin with people and share a culture shift exercise that many communities have found helpful as they are considering change. We will then focus on transforming physical and technology resources.

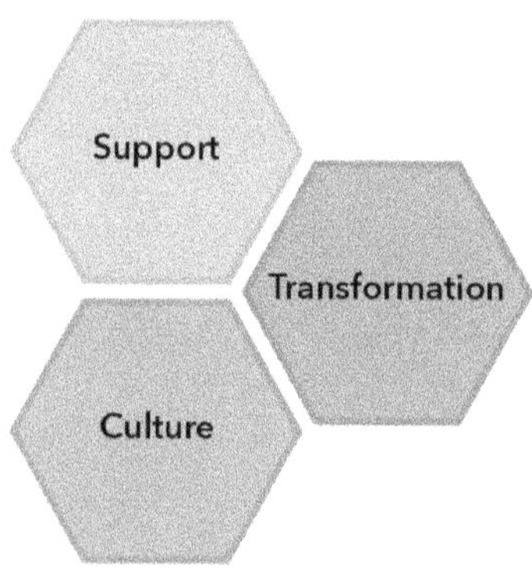

6.1 Cultural Shift Through Teams

A desire to work in teams often represents a significant shift in the culture of an organization. Rather than abruptly making that shift, it can be helpful to first reflect on current practices, envision desired future practices, and co-create a path forward.

6.1.1 Reflecting on Current Practice

When working with schools and communities, we often lead participants through a culture shift exercise that assigns one of each of the 5 elements of culture (Behavior, Artifacts, Language, Traditions, and Stories) to a small team of 3-5 people, with a focus on **current practice**. The current behavior team dives into the details such as the way we divide the school day, organize educators as content-based teams or/and young people into age or ability groups. The **language team** identifies the use of terms such as student, teacher, classmate, teaching, class groups, subjects, grades, and academic reports. The **traditions team** describes proms, graduations, and other celebrations. The **artifacts team** discusses school uniforms, bell systems, certificates, school mottos, school emblems, textbooks, curricular materials, national anthems, etc. The **folklore team** explores the stories we tell about our past, including school songs, the year students rallied the community to act on a global concern, or more recently, the tales of the pandemic.

6.1.2 Envisioning Desired Future Practice

The same elements of culture are assigned to five additional teams with a focus on **desired future practice**. There is a tendency to list current and future practices as dot points. In practice, we have found it helpful for the desired future practice team to share their examples in the form of powerful and memorable stories. Why? Research in behavior science from Walter Mischel (2014), and others confirm that when the desired future practice is dramatically different from the current practice, the desired future practice needs to be vividly described using our "hot" thoughts to trigger positive associations with that future condition. The brain also needs to rationally use our "cool" thoughts to review which current practices will need to be curtailed, honored, and archived in order to redirect our energy into the future vision. For example, it is helpful to acknowledge the careers of many participants who made it possible to arrive at a day when a new future can be envisioned. As noted below, we can honor those efforts without carrying those activities into the future.

6.1.3 Co-Creating Your Cultural Venn Diagram

Each pair of teams comes together to share their observations and create a simple Venn diagram illustrating both the current practices and the desired future practices.

Three types of Venn diagrams might emerge:
- one where the circles fully overlap,
- a second where the circles partially overlap, and
- a third where no overlap is found.

It is rare for a group to create a diagram with complete overlap. Such a diagram would suggest that everything an organization is doing today will continue unchanged into the future. Is what a community really wants? It is also rare for a group to illustrate two distinct circles with no connection between current and future practices. The more common, overlapping diagram (Figure 6.1) reveals three important steps in achieving the desired culture shift.

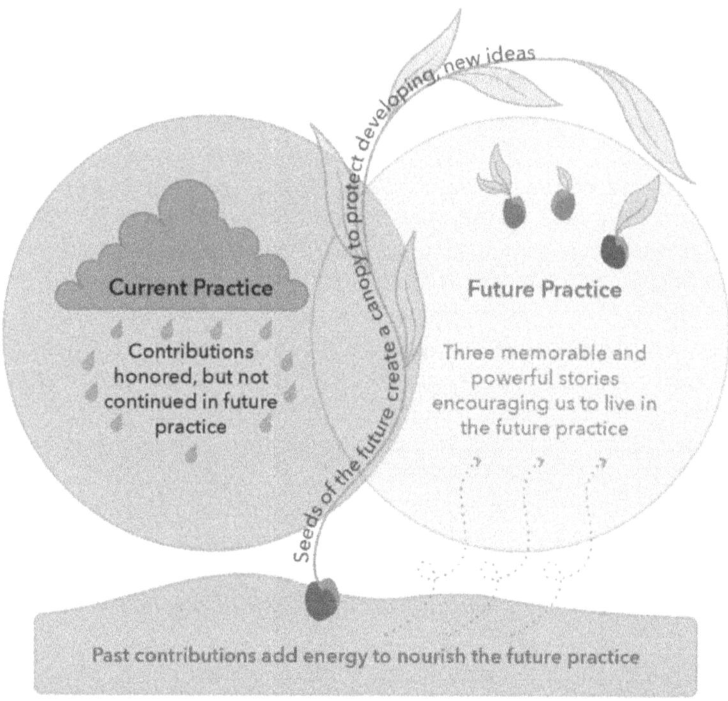

Figure 6.1 teamED Cultural Shift

First, as noted above, sharing the desired future state in the form of powerful, memorable stories, increases the likelihood that the desired future state will be achieved. A participant in the room shared the story and it was heard by others. It is no longer a few words in a report, but a part of the shared, lived experience of the group.

Second, honoring and archiving elements of current practice that are not in the shared zone is important to the people who have invested their energy to get the group to today. Their buy-in of the future vision will be important, dismissing their past contributions will not be an effective path to the desired future state. Individuals and teams in an organization engaging in a cultural shift can now put their energy into the agreed/shared desired future practices.

Finally, the shared zone represents current practices that are a part of the desired future. How might these be nurtured over time to help the group grow into the future vision?

Inspiring Video

Watch PBLWorks (6 Jun 2019). Project-Based Teaching Practices: Build the Culture- Look and Feel of the Classroom 

6.2 Supporting & Sustaining Transformation

Organizations are effectively a team of many teams, as we noted in Chapter 3. What if we envisioned educational institutions and learning communities as part of the firmament that operated as constellations of teams?

6.2.1 Developing a Culture of Teams

Schools work as organizations. In a more traditional school setting, a very hierarchical structure is at work, with leadership styles prone to individual practices. Decisions in hierarchical organizations can be time-consuming as decisions are made, communicated, and confirmed by the person at the top of the pyramid. In this VUCAH world, new approaches are needed. So, what if a school worked as a team of teams organization?

Ashoka Changemakers Schools could be an example of how applying a 'team of teams' organization model could benefit and transform schools. And that is exactly how Bill Drayton (2018) approached the transformation of these schools:

> Instead of maintaining a traditional structure in which people work in hierarchies based on a function or a formal business unit, an organization operates as a constellation of teams that come together around specific goals (Ashoka, 2016. para. 3).

Obviously, it didn't happen overnight, there was a transition. Isn't it the case in many school organizations that come from a more traditional approach in their search for more successful models? What could you learn from their method and the path they have already walked?

For that change to happen, we need to rethink the way individuals, leadership, and teams engage. To start with, we may want to consider educating leaders and teams about the importance of character strengths as the primary driver for a generative culture and ethical innovation (Tilt365). That is a consistent theme that emerged from our interviews with learners, educators, and community partners from around the world: "that everybody has their unique strengths" and that "authentic caring about each other is really foundational", as Lisa Kerscher of Brightways Learning shared (2021).

On top of that, we can get a deeper insight on 'a team of teams' approach, and consider its four design principles from Ashoka (2016):

1. cross-functional / cross-silo participation;
2. evolving and fluid, diffused roles and responsibilities;
3. everyone is empowered to lead thanks to decentralized leadership, decision-making, and execution;
4. and sharing a common vision beyond any individual team member's success.

What would your organization look like if you applied each of them in your specific context?

6.2.2 Nurturing Teams of Teams

Now, consider how the team-of-teams approach might work at a larger scale, for example, in a typical school district. What if they worked as a constellation of teams?

Imagine… Relationship-based teams have the greatest level of connection to young people. Within a single elementary school, there may be 5 or 6 of these teams, with specialists distributed into each team. Those specialists also form a periodic team to address professional learning experiences related to their focus on special education, music, arts, reading, mathematics, phonemic awareness, etc. In addition, some school leaders may choose to distribute administrative resources throughout the building, rather than operating in a separate team.

As we move beyond the team of teams in a single building, we can begin to create and support the growth of a team of teams that connects peers in related roles across a school district, a network of schools, and, why not around the globe?

For that purpose, what can we learn from other fields? From a different angle in the world of politics, business, and the military, General Stanley McChrystal (2015) also referred to a 'team of teams' type of model in his book *Team of Teams* using a similar metaphor, as Figure 6.2 illustrates:

> We looked at the behaviors of our smallest units and found ways to extend them to an organization of thousands, spread across three continents. We became what we called "a team of teams": a large command that captured at scale the traits of agility normally limited to small teams. (p. 29)

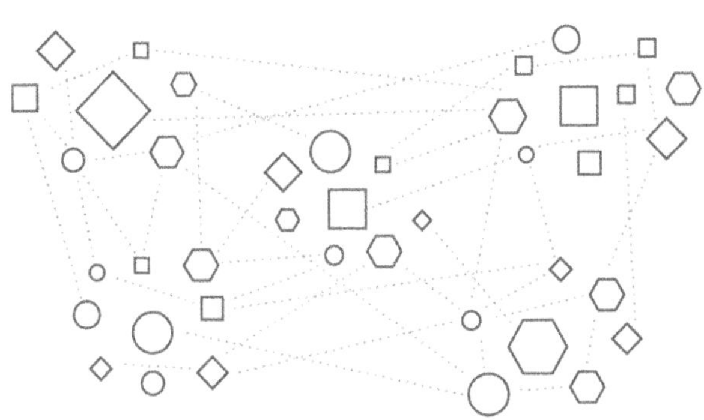

Figure 6.2 Teams of Teams based on McCrystal.

What can we learn then to foster this agility in teams of teams spread over wider communities? Observing each particular context and finding teams that become models for others will help to expand new ways of working with other teams.

A final insight from our research and interviews is that the size of a group is optimized to achieve its focus. For example, a team of educators focuses on creating solid relationships with the learners they work with. That group exports the coordination of teams to another team, the leadership team. Members of the leadership teams are part of a district-wide team tasked with addressing the continuity of relationships between younger and older learners.

The complexity increases as the teams grow in number. But it's not exactly about the numbers. This is why models like the one proposed by Teals organizations (Laloux, 2014) may be worthy of exploring in depth as new organizational methods that operate in a more soulful and purposeful way.

6.2.3 Supporting & Sustaining the Transformation of Teams

As schools and other organizations work to implement and sustain change over time, it may be helpful to think of your first team as plants in a garden nursery in the shared zone of the Culture Shift diagram above (Figure 6.1). The team needs fertile ground to grow. The soil needs to be replenished and watered. Protection from sun, wind and frost may be necessary.

As this team begins to thrive, it may be time to help each person establish new teams, much like dividing lilies and establishing a new bed of flowers, or transplanting trees to new locations where they can thrive. This work should be done with attention to the health of the original team and the potential of each new team. Shall the entire team split and be transplanted all at once? Could a team of four split into two groups, adding new teammates in new settings? Or is one teammate relocated to help develop a team in another setting as the remaining team learns to integrate the perspective of a new teammate?

Just as our gardens are places of experimentation, each of the approaches noted above will yield the best results for that setting and season. In other settings and seasons, different results will be achieved. In the spirit of gardening, our teams are fundamentally learning organizations, adapting to their surroundings.

Pia-Maria Thorén (2019) extends the *garden metaphor* for agile leadership in complex environments; "every garden has a purpose". In that garden, every single plant is unique, has different needs, and plays different roles. And "together, all these plants are fulfilling the purpose of the garden". Doesn't it remind us of a team with very unique members in it? Even more, there is hope for growth in the hardest soils which we can think of. Watch Jeff Duncan-Andrade's "Growing Roses in Concrete" TED Talk, and think about the toughest teams you may have been part of. As Duncan-Andrade states, roses can blossom in concrete, if more water, more light, and more soil are put into it.

In the world of education, we feel "the fierce urgency of now" (NPR, 2023). We cannot afford to wait ten years for trust and connection to be created within a team. But there is no need to put more stress on the shoulders of educators and educational leaders. How can we build trust and connection in a healthier and more sustainable way for everyone? As we noted in Chapter 4, we can accelerate the creation of fertile ground for our team through sharing stories, cooking, singing, laughing, crying, and exploring the world together, so that each new team emerges from a place of trust and deep communication. That place of trust supports celebrations of learning as well as celebrating the arrival of new colleagues and new learners. Just as importantly, we can celebrate the departure of colleagues and learners. In a vibrant team, the majority of the team remains, easing the transition for our peers and for the young people they learn alongside of each day. Young people may have formed a significant bond with a departing educator and can be supported through the transition by the remainder of the team. How we care about the recalibration of these systems is essential. This is why welcoming and onboarding processes are important to team cohesion.

Take a moment and think about your garden or gardens… What is the water, light, and soil for your team? And what fertilizer, nutrients, and care do you need to grow?

6.3. Supporting & Sustaining Transformation Through Cultures of Teaming

As seen in the previous sections, transforming educational organizations implies a shift in their culture that can take a myriad of paths. This third and final approach in this chapter is based on the forces we must truly master to transform schools through the lens of cultures of thinking, according to Ron Ritchhart, researcher at Project Zero Harvard Graduate School of Education. He suggests these 8 forces:

1. Expectations   2. Language 3. Time   4. Modeling
5. Opportunities   6. Routines 7. Interactions 8. Environment

Just as we noted above cultural shift focuses on human beliefs, dispositions, and attitudes, the majority of these eight forces are also focused on human behaviors of expectations, opportunities, routines, interactions, modeling, language, time, and environments. In this section, we are exploring the unique transformational power of each of the 8 forces through the power of teamED.

Ritchhart advocates for transforming schools by nurturing cultures of thinking, where individual and collective thinking are acknowledged, valued, visible, and encouraged. He envisions a school as "a place where the group's collective thinking as well as each individual's thinking was [is] valued, visible, and actively promoted as part of the regular day-to-day experience of all group [and team] members'' (Ritchhart, 2015, p. 3). The power of the group enriches collective thinking, which is otherwise encapsulated in an individual's mind. Ritchhart, Church and Morrison (2011), acknowledge that "within a culture of thinking we want to harness the power of the group to advance general thinking while recognizing the contributions and growth of each individual" (p. 220).

YES AND... Here we go one step further and build on the individual learning process by employing the power of teaming to advance collective thinking and learning. Every individual contribution and development as a team member is important. Imagine if you embraced a transformational approach from these cultures of thinking and teaming. What if your organization creates opportunities to develop cultures of teaming, where individual and collective thinking are acknowledged, valued, visible, and encouraged, and where everyone could feel they truly belong to a community?

6.3.1 Transformation Through Expectations, Opportunities & Routines

Expectations. To start, there is a need to explore and develop expectations (or co-created team agreements) you and your team have co-created while transforming education in a particular context. In the light of Ritchhart's approach, expectations include a set of beliefs which shape our behavior, and they give rise to actions that result in certain outcomes (Ritchhart, 2015, p. 43). We ascribe to them all and also want to emphasize the following ones as essential for our purpose:

- Nurturing a growth, benefit, or even, an agile mindset in contrast to a fixed one, as we already discussed in chapter 5.1. This way we are making room to think that the power of the collective intelligence in a team may, and will, enrich learning in multiple ways.
- Encouraging not only independent learners, that are "internally motivated to be reflective, resourceful, and effective as they strive to accomplish worthwhile endeavors when working in isolation or with others" (Rose-Duckworth & Ramer, 2008, p. 2), but also fostering positive interdependence when working with others to collaborate successfully in teams.
- Considering mistakes as opportunities to learn, to grow, to rethink, and to iterate. The team integrates feed-up, feedback, and feed-forward (Hattie & Timperley, 2007) focused on the learning, not on the learner.

Opportunities. Think, recognize and co-design learning opportunities where mistakes are embraced, and most importantly, learning opportunities where every single learner is and feels included. For this purpose, we consider the Universal Design for Learning framework (CAST, 2024), together with its principles, framework and guidelines to meet individual needs, so that they can also shine as members in any team:

> The UDL Guidelines are a tool used in the implementation of Universal Design for Learning. These guidelines offer a set of concrete suggestions that can be applied to any discipline or domain to ensure that all learners can access and participate in meaningful, challenging learning opportunities (para. 5).

Being part of a team may be a challenging learning opportunity indeed.

Routines. When we think of routines, we are not only considering typical classroom management routines, but visible thinking routines (VTR): tools, structures, and patterns, that allow every team member's thinking to be visible and foster positive collaboration. Although we have mentioned a few VTR previously in chapter 5.3, we are sharing some particular examples to nurture the soil where the seeds of teams may grow. Ideally, the entire team is aware of these routines, speaks the same shared language, and engages in strategies to develop both individual and collective thinking. Why not start by trying these VTR?

Think-Pair-Share - Listening to and sharing ideas, promotes understanding through active reasoning and explanation, as well as understanding multiple perspectives.

Circle of viewpoints - Promotes seeing and exploring multiple perspectives.

Lenses - Although initially engaged to explore an artwork, it supports being intentional about looking through distinct lenses when

exploring a particular issue, object, idea, etc. It is useful as a reminder that our lenses are affected by our identities or backgrounds.
What makes you say that? - Explores evidence-based reasoning and encourages understanding alternatives and multiple perspectives.

If you want to dig deeper into these, and other visible thinking routines, check the complete *Thinking Routines Toolbox* from Project Zero (2022).

6.3.2 Transformation Through Interactions, Modeling & Language

Interactions. When working in teams, interactions can become an issue if not handled properly from the beginning. A warning light may turn on in our brains thinking of a previous unsuccessful experience. For instance, have you ever been in a team where only a few members committed to their tasks, and ended up doing someone else's work too? It may happen among the leaders in a school board, educators, and learners of any age. Obviously, working in teams has its challenges and dangers, this is why we shared numerous strategies with you in Chapter 4.

In our interactions, we focus on those that empower any individual when performing a new role. Interactions may come from the roles of recorder, reporter, or reflector; but also, from interactions that support thinking, deeper learning, and interconnectedness in a team with aspirations to develop team members, and/or team leaders.

> A culture will be strong or weak depending on the interactions between people in the organization. In a strong culture, there are many, overlapping, and cohesive interactions, so that knowledge about the organization's distinctive character— and what it takes to thrive in it— is widely spread (Schafer, 2018, para. 5).

Teaming also provides the framework to increase peer-to-peer interactions where peer learning flourishes beyond the traditionally ingrained teacher-student interactions. Team practices that build upon each other's ideas are a must for constructive collaboration. The visually powerful 'Popcorn vs Ice-cream' metaphor is a clear example (Ritchhart, 2015). When popcorning everyone involved in a conversation is just shouting out their own ideas, without necessarily caring about and listening to others' ideas. Our ego may cause us to be right, to be clever, and on top of others. On the contrary, when we practice 'ice-creaming', we add scoops in the same ice cream cone, which melt and fuse into a collective contribution. When we elaborate on each other's ideas, we find part of what someone else has shared and connect it to our own ideas.

Modeling. Teaming can be also modeled, and teams of educators can be a good example for learners when working in teams. In this way, we also foster the independence of learners when in teams. Learning will not come only from modeling, but also from examples, practice, and reflection. Modeling and learning through examples mean learners will learn from seeing teams in action, and also from being engaged in action, rather than just words. Let's be coherent. Learners learn from educators, for good or bad, and they also learn from school leaders.

As Klein and Ciotti (2002) suggest, leaders need to do with teachers what they want to see teachers do with students; and this may end up becoming a powerful form of professional learning by constantly modeling what educators want to see happening in the classrooms (p. 213). What if learners see examples of effective and successful teamwork daily? What if school leaders and teachers create a community of practice where collaboration with each other is openly shared before the learners' eyes and ears?

Language. Language can profoundly shape the way we think (Boroditsky, 2018), interact, and create a sense of belonging to a team and a wider community. From the set of languages considered by Ritchhart (2015), we have chosen a few examples to increase awareness of our team-oriented language:

- **language of community.** What if we prioritize the words 'we', 'our', 'us'? These words of sharing and inclusion enhance a feeling of belonging to a team and to a wider community and a feeling of shared ownership.
- **language of identity.** What if we take specific roles and name them? Learners can be identified as team members, team leaders, thinkers, listeners, communicators, problem solvers, change-makers, etc.
- **language of listening.** What if team members listen for understanding? As we already mentioned in section 4, listening for understanding rather than for judging other's ideas may show respect for others and interest in others, opening up for valuing each others' perspectives.
- **language of praise & feedback**. What if we routinely praise our team members by drawing attention to a teammate's effort and action? This type of feedback may enhance positive relationships and team growth by encouraging ongoing learning, embracing challenges, and taking risks. What if team members get used to giving and receiving feedback among themselves using diverse techniques, such as the following one:
  1. making specific comments on what a team member has done well;
  2. pointing out 2 aspects a team member must work on to improve and move forward;
  3. elaborating on a positive statement on growth, progress, and effort.
- **language of mindfulness.** What if we use conditional language rather than absolute language? Using conditional language may open up possibilities for everyone else in a team to participate and share their voices and perspectives, and to think more critically.

6.3.3 Transformation Through Time and Environments

Time. What if you could make a small investment in time today that would increase the time available to complete a project by a factor of 5? That is the power of slowing down to build your team and experience the benefits of teamwork. When we invest time at the beginning of a school year to co-create agreements and ways of working in teams, we see the return on that investment in the form of flow when working in teams throughout the school year, dismantling the belief that working in collaborative teams takes more time than working individually. The resulting learning and outcomes are greater than the sum of the parts.

For example, when we work in a jigsaw format, 5 teams can each contribute to the collective understanding of the group, completing a project in less time. Anytime you are tempted to spend weeks researching and planning a project, ask yourself- "Could this be done more effectively and more deeply if we captured the power of our teams?" Terry Doyle (2023) of Ferris State University reminds us that "The one who does the work does the learning" (p.7). Stated in another way, are we robbing a team of young people of opportunities to learn when we spend late-night hours doing the same work?

The more time we spend working with schools, the more we are convinced that one of the most revolutionary things any school could do is to establish new priorities about how we spend our time together, and it doesn't cost a penny to implement!

The Team Challenge: "Timetabling for Deeper Learning" described below offers an opportunity to take on the challenge of how your team uses time for discussions, meetings, learning, and time to develop as a team. You might take up this exercise as a fast, iterative learning cycle, borrowed from Agile Learning and eduScrum.

The exercise helps communities focus on how the school day and calendar can be organized to support highly effective learning experiences. Most schools are organized around the convenience of adults, not what is best for learners. The daily, weekly, and annual schedule is often the greatest challenge to flexibility and innovation. Many educators would argue that the typical school schedule is not very convenient for adults either.

The exercise begins by dividing into mixed groups of young people, educators, and community partners into three or more groups, each focusing on a few of the questions below.

GROUP 1:

A. What time of day should the school day begin? How long should the school day be?
B. Why does the schedule on Monday look the same as Tuesday, Wednesday, Thursday, and Friday?
C. Why does the school day need to start and end at the same time for everyone?
D. Why do bells and chimes persist in our schools and how else could we mark transition periods?

GROUP 2:

E. What would learners tell us about their experience of school?
F. How long should class periods be?
G. Why do we need class periods?
H. How can common planning time for teachers and staff be introduced into every school day?

GROUP 3:

I. What alternatives to the lunch bottleneck can be implemented? How might we slow down the dining experience?
J. How long should the school year be and how should the school year be divided?
K. When considering the long summer break, what works? What could be better? What's missing?
L. What did we learn from the COVID-19 pandemic about how we might structure time?

M. How can we be purposeful about the time we spend together face-to-face?

Each group identifies a spokesperson who shares the highlights of the small group discussion with the whole group. Participants wrap up this challenge with the statement of a **Guiding Principle**, for example, "Common planning time for teams of 4-5 teachers/staff every day can be achieved while learners are engaged in exploratory programs in art, music, physical education and applied learning."

Once this foundational exercise has taken place, it is possible to dive more deeply into the next exercise, "Scheduling for Deeper Learning." Why not take your turn at this challenge?

Team Challenge: Timetabling for Deeper Learning
The daily, weekly/fortnight, term, and annual calendars often create barriers to innovation and will require additional exploration. A study group examining the impacts of the timetable on deeper learning might consider many concepts from BAU (Business As Usual) to SOS (Start Over Schedule)

OPTION BAU Business As Usual
No Changes to Existing Daily, Weekly, Fortnight, Term or Annual Schedule

OPTION IWS Innovation Within Structure
Two educators working with the same learners in two consecutive periods simply ignore the bell to create a longer block of time dedicated to interdisciplinary areas of study

OPTION IFR Innovation with Fortnight Rotation (Or Month/ Term)
Over the course of two weeks, the daily timetable would include a traditional daily schedule with longer blocks of time, culminating in a potentially non-scheduled day (or week) where learners work independently, seeking coaching from educators as needed.

OPTION IWW Innovation Within a Week
Over the course of a week, the daily timetable would include a traditional daily schedule with longer blocks of time, culminating in a potentially non-scheduled day where learners work independently, seeking coaching from educators as needed.

OPTION SOS Start Over Schedule
Over the course of a year, the daily timetable would include a traditional daily schedule with varied blocks of time, and weeks of un-scheduled days where learners work independently, seeking coaching from educators as needed. A term might begin with "Deep Dives" into interdisciplinary projects or "Cannonballs" of projects linking many Key Learning Areas (Science, Math, Language Arts, History) and Applied Learning Areas (Music, Art, VET, etc.)

Each of these concepts (and more) are developed with input from learners, educators, and community partners. Each option can be studied using the 'What Works?' Framework, identifying What Works? What Could Be Better? and What's Missing? for each option. That feedback can be used to improve each option.

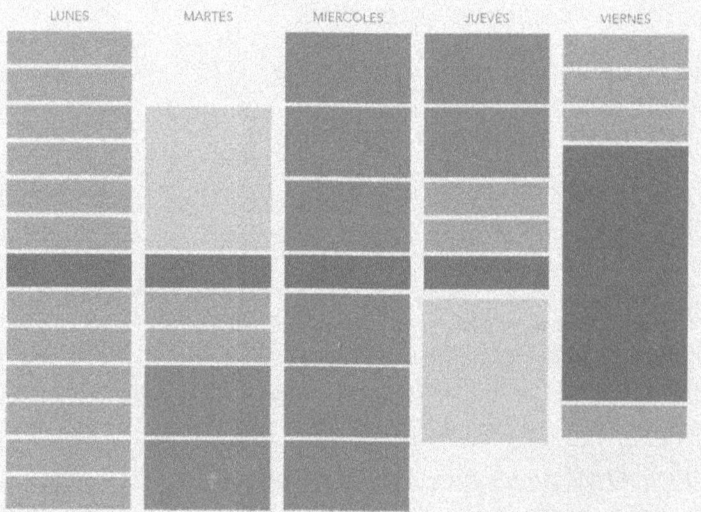

The options can also be reviewed using Guiding Principles developed by learners, educators, and community partners such as:

- Creates opportunities for interdisciplinary learning.
- Creates blocks of time for a mix of direct instruction and hands-on creation of evidence of learning.
- Creates adequate blocks of time for on-site and off-site work experiences.
- Creates time to begin and end the day together.
- Creates time for community partners to be a part of learning experiences.

Additional Resources: Dynamic Governance
The process of Dynamic Governance was developed in the Netherlands following the chaos and destruction of the Second World War and has been used by groups seeking to empower all decision-makers and to arrive at decisions that have deep levels of buy-in.

A typical meeting is organized as follows:

Opening Round. *Establishing the "We" Used for checking-in; sharing with the group your transition from where you've been and an opportunity to state the baggage you're carrying about any agenda items, for example, "I am really looking forward to our time together" or " I just had an upsetting call from a parent" or "I have concerns about a specific item on the agenda."*
Administrative Matters. *Taking Care of Team Health.*
Agenda Adjustments. *(based upon check-in/ opening round).*
Schedule Next Meeting. *(rather than waiting to the end of the meeting). See also, The Art of Gathering by Priya Parker, and the importance of not ending on logistics.*
Matters of Content. *focuses on Team Working on Its Aim.*
Clear proposals. *Proposals generally are organized as a recommendation from a team, task force, or individual. Seek consent within the range of tolerance of the group.*
Issue needing to be unraveled. *The situation is not entirely clear or impacts many aspects of operations. Identify and unravel overlapping issues, and clarify which are most important to address. Seek volunteers to develop a clear proposal.*
Team Reports. *Keep track of Team activities; ensure that Teams have adequate resources and are doing their work.*
Closing Round. *Evaluation of Meeting Leadership & Teamwork Used to evaluate facilitation of meetings and teamwork during meetings. For example "I feel that keeping our agenda tight today really helped us to explore this one issue more deeply" or "That was hard work, but I am glad we spent time talking about the elephant in the room" or "I am grateful for the support you each provided this morning."*

Environments (physical, online, and hybrid)

"We shape our buildings, thereafter they shape us"
-Winston Churchill, British Prime Minister (October 28, 1944)

"Let's change setting, let's change medium, let's change our dynamic, we're together, we're apart—options that were just so natural in a physical space, all those things that kept people's creativity and energy and relationships going were just vaporized, and teams couldn't immediately, figure it out how to do it differently"
-Ela Ben-Ur, Innovators Compass. Cambridge, Massachusetts (2022)

We can create environments to enhance learning where individuals and teams can find their place. In many cases, learning environments around the world do a great job of keeping people apart. Although we have spent time in tens of thousands of learning environments around the world, each space reinforces a similar pattern: working alone in an isolated box, solving all the problems of the universe in a room that looks like every other room with minor exceptions made for music, physical education, and career technology- spaces that reinforce the isolated practice of teaching and learning. Typical learning environments include built-in (and expensive) storage cabinets, a sink, a "teaching wall" and thankfully, in most cases, a window wall. What takes place in one box is unrelated to what takes place in an adjacent box.

School designers frequently refer to the efficiency of a "double-loaded corridor" planning scheme, ignoring that 25-40% of the building is dedicated to single-purpose circulation. More than 5% of a typical classroom is taken up by the highly inflexible cabinets. Those same cabinets also reduce the surface area that could be dedicated to displaying the learning process. 10% to 30% of the space is allocated to the "teacher zone" in the form of a battleship-sized desk positioned to claim the territory at the "front of the room" as belonging to the educator. A typical school allocates ownership of each of these learning environments to an individual, reducing the utilization of the space significantly when considering individual and common planning time woven into the daily timetable.

The utilization of the learning environment drops precipitously when considering that a school is occupied about 8 hours a day and about half of each year. The result is that for a school of 100,000 square feet, the net utilization is less than 10,000 square feet. Not a very good return on the substantial investment most communities make in their schools. We can do better.

Figure 6.3 Small Learning Communities, Chicago Heights, USA (2024) Photo by Nick Salmon

Small Learning Communities & Extended Learning Areas

The first step is to break away from the assumption that educators, and learners, work alone. A small group of adults (4-6) sharing responsibility for the development of 120-150 learners need a greater variety of learning environments, beginning with a place to gather, work on projects, make presentations, share technology (and perhaps dine in small groups). These "Extended Learning Areas" can be created by folding a typical corridor upon itself to create a usable space in the heart of each Small Learning Community.

That extended learning doesn't work for our most introverted learners, and as a result, small group rooms should be located nearby. If these rooms are separated using walls of glass, occupants can still connect with their peers while finding the scale and acoustical environment that works best for their learning.

Link to Outdoor Learning

The extended learning area should be connected to outdoor learning spaces with overhead shade and rain protection. Ideally, these outdoor learning environments vary in orientation; some to the North, South, East, and West, supporting use at various times of day and year in nearly all climates.

Figure 6.4 School in Siirt, Turkey (2012) Photo by Mar Cano

Figure 6.5 *Congrés d'Indians* School. Barcelona, Catalonia, Spain (2018). Photo by Mar Cano

Planning Centers

The next key element of a small learning community could be a collaborative planning center or home base for the adults who work together each day. This eliminates the need for individual teacher desks in each classroom, allowing smaller learning environments without sacrificing any space. The planning center should have a table, comfortable chairs on casters, a sink, refrigerator, microwave, and coffee pot to support planning, dining, laughing, and personal phone calls. The planning center is highly visible to the extended learning area so that learners see adults collaborating, and adults provide passive supervision of the extended learning area.

Figure 6.6 Collaborative Planning Center. SAMI. Tacoma, Washington (2018). Photo by Nick Salmon

The planning center may include simple storage lockers for personal items, including a few spares for substitute teachers, grandparent volunteers, and other specialists. Imagine how different your day would be as a substitute educator if you began with a quick huddle with your new teammates.

Shared Storage

Another key space is a simple storage closet, 8 feet wide by as deep as you can make it, perhaps 20-30 feet. Simple metal shelves from floor to ceiling with a place to park a supply cart when transferring materials for the week from storage to the various learning environments. An advantage of open shelving (besides the low cost) is the ability to survey the contents of the shelves, rather than the tedious task of opening and closing cabinet doors one by one until giving up on finding what you are seeking. The scale of sharing is important. This cannot become a closet accessible to the entire school, but instead for the small learning community team.

Variety of Learning Environments

A variety of learning environments surrounding an extended learning area reinforce the notion that all of the resources are available to all learners and educators based upon the particular learning needs for that portion of the day, week, month or year. If educators have a home base in the form of the planning center, learning environments no longer need to belong to individuals, but rather the entire learning community. The variety of learning environments typically includes conference-sized rooms, medium and large rooms, and flexible labs capable of accommodating art, science, robotics, fabrication, culinary programs, and events.

Figure 6.7 *Congrés d'Indians* School. Barcelona, Catalonia, Spain (2018). Photo by Mar Cano

In the United States, the inclusion model for special education has been the law of the land for more than 30 years, yet we routinely see exclusionary practices in schools. The small learning community becomes the logical extension of the inclusion model of special education where the occasional pull-out for learning support takes place within the community rather than in a stand-alone setting.

Other Voices

"The environment is critical to the teamwork… in my classroom, our day always begins in a circle, because that allows us to see each other connect with each other and build relationship."
- Louise Whitaker, Primary School Educator, Macquarie College. Wallsend, Australia (2022)

"We created the environment for collaborative work as well, because the school year would start with a blank wall. And then there would be things displayed on the wall, from the children, but also, the design of the display was not exclusively designed by myself, or by the teaching assistants on their own. It was normally a collaborative effort."
- Kavita Tanna, Catalyst Learning Labs, Global (2022)

Group Security

A frequent resistance to the transparency and connection between learning environments as described in this section is a concern for safety, specifically how safety is provided during an armed intrusion. Safety is provided at the scale of the community rather than room-by-room. More importantly, the connection between the extended learning area and outdoor learning provides a means of evacuation that does not expose learners and educators to potential harm in a typical building corridor. This approach works for ground-level communities and those located on a second or third level.

Thoughtful planning of security doors has additional benefits of providing fire separations and limiting access to the small learning community after-hours to allow custodial staff to complete their work one time without repeatedly cleaning areas as after-school programs occupy the building. Access to restrooms can be maintained during a lockdown and can be isolated or accessible after-hours matching after-school program needs.

Online and Virtual Environments

The pandemic offered new ways of thinking about the transformation of learning and organization of our learning environments, no longer constrained by the four walls of a typical classroom or the hours of the school day. For example, educators who might make the same presentation 6 or 8 times a day, could record that presentation once, and share it with learners and their families to be viewed as many times as necessary. Many educators extended that practice in the post-pandemic setting, freeing up class time for a deeper exploration of the concepts shared in the video.

As Ela Ben Ur of Innovators Compass notes about the use of chat functions in video meetings, *"We would not have had it (chat) if you're facilitating a live workshop, it would be like texting to each other, like in front of this audience. So that has been really cool to be able to communicate at two different levels and two different ways of people at the same time has been really really neat."* Because the chat function can be saved on most video call platforms, those exchanges can become a part of the reflection practices of any group.

Other Voices

"Technology was paramount in keeping that connection with my students and maintaining their well-being and their education and all of those things during the pandemic."
- Louise Whitaker, Primary School Educator, Macquarie College.
Wallsend, Australia (2022)

When we examined team sizes and types in Chapter 3, we noted a series of insights about 'Virtual Teams and Hybrid Teams.' Those insights included our conversation with Suzie Boss which spanned the connection between technology and culture, specifically during the pandemic.

> **Other Voices**
>
> "My team project during the pandemic was working with Ken Kay to write a book. We did all our research and writing during the pandemic- just a team of two, working with the publisher. But it taught me a lot because we were interviewing school leaders and teachers who were in the middle of the pandemic and trying to adapt. And even though we had questions beyond that, that was where they wanted to start the conversation because that was their reality. We learned a lot about the need to broadly

generalize the school system that seemed to be able to keep their focus on really important goals during the pandemic, and keep moving toward those. The ones that did not have really strong culture in place before the pandemic, if they didn't have that culture, if they weren't able to tolerate risk taking or innovation or really caring about everybody's well being, if that wasn't part of the culture, where the pandemic really hit hard, they were stymied, when it came to solutions. Then they would fall back on really traditional practices, and then kids would suffer because they're back to worksheets, they're just doing them online.

In contrast, in the districts that had a really strong culture, they had a clear vision, they were able to make progress without feeling like the pandemic put a halt to anything creative or innovative in their ability to work with kids. It wasn't perfect, but they could problem solve, they can trust each other to try things. And they had that sense, throughout, from leadership on through their teams, that it's okay, if it's not perfect, you know, we're gonna learn from what we try, we're in this crisis. And if we don't try new things, we're not going to get through it. So we're not expecting perfection.

For example, if you're a district that has some kids who have access to technology, and some don't, you can't do online learning for everybody. So what, what's our work around? How do we come up with that? Instead of just saying, Oh, we can't reach our kids? These are the districts that got creative and thought, Okay, well, we're going to find out who has access, who doesn't? How do we reach those? Who are furthest from opportunity? How do we get maybe materials to them, things that they can do in and around their neighborhoods? So that culture was just really critical to the success of districts that have been able to survive, and you know, moving toward, we hope coming out of this at some point without feeling like they've gone back 20 years in their teaching and learning practices. That's a big fear that everybody reverts when it gets hard, you revert to what you know, and what's easiest, and that's not always the best for kids."

-Suzie Boss, Author of 12 books on Project-Based Learning and
innovation in education (Portland, Oregon)

During the global pandemic, Nick joined Kavita Tanna to participate in two online graduate school of education courses taught by Dr. Elizabeth Crawford at the University of North Carolina, Wilmington. Dr. Crawford is a master of engaging up to 30 learners using padlets, chat functions, breakout rooms and whole group discussions. Her work demonstrates that online learning environments can establish meaningful connections between participants leading to the formation of online teams.

School leaders in New South Wales began an online meeting with Nick with a long list of positive experiences and insights from the pandemic that they will extend into face-to-face learning experiences including deepening relationships and connections with learners and families; integrating digital resources into learning experiences; providing opportunities for parents to participate in learning experiences through technology; conducting learner-led conferences with parents online; conducting interviews with community partners live streaming events; addressing the wellbeing of learners, families, educators and community partners; integrating more flexibility into the daily timetable and considering new ways to document and share the outcomes of the learning process.

During the post-pandemic, Mar has also experienced different kinds of learning experiences with kids, teenagers, educators, professors, etc. In each case, all the experiences led to different types of teams. Moreover, it has been very powerful to experience how online learning environments can allow more flexibility when it comes to creating and managing teams. It is not much about the size or the type, but it is more about a whole community sharing a common goal, e.g. kids from every corner of the world hacking the current crisis from five approaches in Kids Hack the Crisis, to teams of teenagers competing to solve EduCaixa Challenges as changemakers, or to Spanish educators trying to solve ten challenges derived from the Covid-19 pandemic in La Escuela lo Primero.

Your Turn: Are large online groups really teams? Or are they just groups only sharing space, time, and activities? Think about the experiences you may have taken part in, particularly during the pandemic, and reflect on the role of technology in the different teams you may have been a member of.

__A quick furniture whispering recommendation-__
Place the video camera midway on the long side of a room so that all participants can be seen and heard. Many video conference rooms we work with do exactly the opposite- the video camera is on the short side of the room/table resulting in being able to hear (but not see) those people closest to the video source and see (but not hear) people seated at the far end of the table.

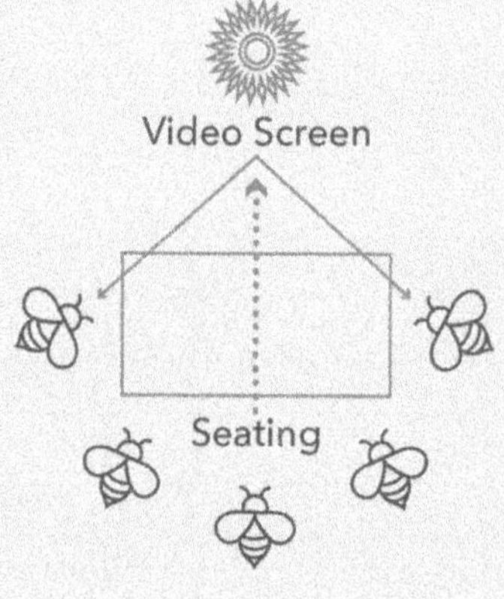

Before the pandemic, a typical educational visioning workshop would be conducted over multiple days, 6-8 hours each. We were asked what could be achieved in 4 hours, or even 2 hours. As a result, we shifted to a jigsaw method of workshops, where each table team was engaged in a different exercise. This dramatically improved the depth of exploration, when each team knew they were the only ones exploring relationships, time, technology, etc. We continued this approach throughout the pandemic and found new advantages of sharing documents where everyone's contributions could be captured, rather than the one person who took charge of the marker and chart paper.

As many of us learned during numerous video calls, we could use chat functions to check in, share thoughts, and retain a record of both the video, audio, and group chat in ways we could not in conventional team settings. As digital technology changed throughout the pandemic, new tools emerged, and new collaborative platforms were added, stretching individuals and teammates to return to the cycle of Accelerating Awareness, Building Credibility, Developing Insight, and Sharing Wisdom.

Team Challenge: Technology Integration

This exercise focuses on how technology is transforming learning beyond a "go-to" event, scheduled in a computer lab, to support anytime, anyplace learning. The mobile nature of technology is often not deployed effectively, resulting in tablets and laptops that are utilized in fixed lab settings.

Nearly universal access to information has eliminated the need to retain and recall facts but increased the demand to evaluate often conflicting sources of information.

QUESTIONS

Identify a recorder for your group. Note your responses on a large sheet of paper.

GROUP 1:

    A. *How can we support sending technology home with students every day when access to technology at home may not be equitable?*

    B. *What technology do we need to allow learners to create as well as receive content?*

C. What types of professional development are needed to get your teaching staff up to speed and to sustain that momentum once in place?

GROUP 2:
D. How can a team of teachers and learners share technology resources without the "computer lab" approach to technology?
E. Why is 1:1 technology desirable, why not 3-5 devices: 1 user or 1 device: 3 users or no technology?
F. How do we maintain online safety yet provide access to real-world experiences?
G. How can world language, math, language arts, PE, CTE, and other classes be offered entirely online?

GROUP 3:
H. What technology do we need to meet periodic standardized testing requirements and does it need to be permanent?
I. How can we make the best use of the mobile nature of technology?
J. If students have 24/7 access to information, lessons, lectures, tutors, etc, why do they need to come to school?
K. What does learning look like during technology holidays?
L. What impact do station rotations, blended learning, and flipped classrooms have on the organization and quantity of learning environments?

GROUP 4:
M. What lessons did we learn during the global Pandemic about our use of technology?
N. What would learners tell us about our use of technology?
O. What would community partners tell us about our use of technology?

Identify a spokesperson for your group, and share the highlights of your discussion with the whole group.

Identify Guiding Principles, for example, "Technology is distributed throughout buildings with portable and flexible equipment supported by robust wireless access to support critical thinking, communication, collaboration and creativity."

Digital tools for equity, inclusivity, and personalization

Every team is composed of diverse members with different experiences with digital technology and ways of accessing information, expressing ideas, and engaging as a team. It is helpful to agree on the tools you will use according to the preferences of your team.

The more digital tools we have in our toolbox, the more chances we may have to find a tool we all may be comfortable with. Encourage your teammates to try a new tool and discover what tool works for the task at hand. The tools may change as your team's purposes shift along the way.

Your Turn: What digital tool(s) would you like to try now to help you in teamwork? Why would you choose that one or those ones?

Other Voices

"La comunicación fue diversa, en especial mediante algunas herramientas digitales como: Jamboard, Filpgrid, Kialo Edu, entre otras."

"Communication was diverse, especially with some digital tools like Jamboard, Filpgrid, Kialo Edu, among others."

- Milton Javier Pirazán Rodríguez, Docente, Departamento de Humanidades y Formación Integral. UAD/ Facultad de educación, Universidad Santo Tomás. Tunja, Colombia (2022)

Collaboration tools like the ones Milton Javier Pirazán Rodríguez describes above increase the participation of introverted collaborators, particularly when the contributions can be anonymous. In a face-to-face session, a quieter voice might not be heard in the flow of a conversation.

Other Voices

"todo fue en escenarios virtuales, algunos colaborativos sincrónicos y de opinión asincrónicos."

"everything was in virtual environments, some collaborative synchronous and asynchronous opinions"

- John Franklin Castro Arévalo, Docente, Licenciatura en Artes Plasticas, DUAD/ Facultad de educación, Universidad Santo Tomás. Tunja, Colombia (2022)

The asynchronous opportunities found in virtual environments create time for additional reflection and a return to discussions when each participant is best able to contribute.

Virtual environments opened the door for collaboration between educators who could now join their peers online as needed, share videos of presentations, and seek feedback on their practice. The same door blurs the line between school and community, increasing the accessibility of community resources, available anywhere in the world.

The safety of young people remains a concern in a virtual environment where people, trolls and AI add to the complexity of understanding who you are connecting with, but each presents opportunities for authentic learning experiences where young people learn to connect to adults through research, email introductions or simple phone calls.

Digital portfolios, a future dream for many learners and educators, quickly became a reality during the pandemic, with every artifact of learning made visible to our peers. Educator portfolios are more frequently integrated into teacher's professional learning.

Other Voices

"Influyó mucho, teniendo en cuenta las clases mediadas por tecnología que facilitaron la implementación de nuevas herramientas digitales para el trabajo en equipo y colaborativo que generó un dinámica y motivación en los estudiantes mayor y la satisfacción de elegir lo más apropiado en su proceso de aprendizaje."

"It influenced a lot, considering classes mediated by technology which facilitated the implementation of new digital tools to work in teams and collaboratively which increased a higher dynamic and motivation in the students and the satisfaction to choose the most appropriate in their learning process."

- Milton Javier Pirazán Rodríguez (2022)

"Estuve más tranquilo trabajando virtualmente desde mi casa. aprendí cosas nuevas, disciplina, horarios, descansos, familia y trabajo"
"I was calmer working virtually from home. I learned new things, discipline, scheduling, breaks, family and work"

"Ohh, muchas opciones con las nuevas herramientas para trabajar sincrónica y asincrónicamente de formas más creativas."
"Ohh, many options with new tools to work synchronously and asynchronously in creative ways"

- John Franklin Castro Arévalo (2022)

Hybrid Environments

One of the most challenging environments for teaching and learning during the pandemic was a hybrid of face-to-face and online participants. In some cases, hybrid teaching and learning was underway well before the pandemic, often in rural communities where an educator might be face-to-face with a group of young people in one setting while engaging with individuals and small groups in other settings. Hybrid work environments crossing time zones and continents have become increasingly common. As hybrid practices endure, we can ask "How can we best create a unified experience for everyone?"

"The composition of many meetings will be a random mix of in-person, on-video, and dialed-in participants. And that is going to make it more difficult for leaders to "figure out how to manage dynamics, keep the conversation going, and make it inclusive," says Albertina Vaughn, a senior client partner in Korn Ferry's Leadership and Professional Development group" (2021, para. 4). Vaughn recommends five keys to a successful hybrid team environment, expanded with our own observations:
1. **Don't go in cold.** Have a plan for how the time will be spent, check the placement of face-to-face cameras and microphones so that online participants can see/hear everyone in the room.
2. **Balance the ratio** of face-to-face and online participants so that neither group dominates the conversation.
3. **Get everyone involved** to develop protocols for check-ins that include every participant, including the facilitators.
4. **Double up facilitation.** One facilitator may have greater skill managing the technology, or "reading the room" as the conversation unfolds.
5. **Purposeful breakout sessions**. Continuing to blend the face-to-face participants with online teammates. Leave enough time to check in within the small group, recorder, reporter, and reflector roles, affirm access to shared technology (Miro boards, Google Docs, etc) time available, and desired outcome (Manson-Smith, et.al., 2021, para. 8-12).

Hybrid Learning Environments provide opportunities to revisit the much-maligned open classrooms of the late 1960's and early 1970's, and to improve upon the design of learning communities to include diverse learning environments with a variety of room sizes, levels of transparency, lighting, and color.

> Open classrooms are often blamed for being built to fit *extroverts*. Remote work, on the other hand, is often described as being the perfect fit for ***introverts***, with its possibilities for choosing a calm place to work or study where you can focus on one thing at a time, in your own time. In a remote setting, we are in many ways better set up to cater to both needs by using **asynchronous work** to give time for reflection, and **synchronous work to give** space to spontaneity and on-the-spot thinking." (The Hows Online Facilitation Masterclass. Kids hack Day Academy).

We can amend Winston Churchill's quote that began this focus on environments to state: "We shape our hybrid learning environments, thereafter they shape the way we work as teams."

Transforming the way you use time as a team, expanding your cultures of thinking, and thinking differently about the many environments your team works within all contribute to your continued growth as a team. As you build confidence to fully participate in your personal and collective transformation, as an educator, project team or community leader, you will quickly see opportunities to call your peers and community to action. And that is precisely where we will wrap up this exploration of the power of teams.

CHAPTER 7: REFLECTION, INSPIRATION & ACTION
Awareness, Advocacy and Action

"Everyone has something to offer. No one has nothing. No one has everything. None of us exists alone."
– Rose Poka,, Emerging Leader Representative-Duke of Edinburgh International Award-Africa. Nakuru, Kenya (2021)

"We become Agents of transformation when we develop Awareness, we engage in Advocacy and ultimately, take Action."
– Kavita Tanna, Catalyst Learning Labs. Global (2022)

One of the most revolutionary things we can do in education is to work together, and it doesn't cost a penny to implement. Each of us has a role in creating our team, working through the challenges, and embracing the opportunities to nurture and grow the culture of our team. As you do that work, share your experiences with your peers, with our team, and with the world; you will be helping to shape the future of teams and to shape the future of a better world.

Our call to action is urgent for each of us. Our peers who were already practicing in isolation struggled much more during the pandemic. If they returned to teaching (many did not), they would have fewer resources to address their own well-being and the well-being of the young people they work with.

People continue to be inspired to become educators. How might we support their growth as educators through the team practices we have shared with you throughout this book?

The territory varies from place to place, but the journey is similar. Begin with building trust, purpose, and solid communication. With that foundation, you can identify the skills needed for your team to succeed. Trust is also required to provide an honest self-assessment of your strengths and challenges to contribute to the team. As you develop your team, return to the wide range of successful practices we shared– listening, laughing, and learning together. You will have the confidence to make decisions large and small, to use restorative practices to address conflict, and work through challenges together. As you build confidence as a team, you will find that your current educational practices become more effective, and new practices become easier to embrace, whether they are agile, project-based, thinking-based, or future practices none of us can yet imagine. If you are well on your way to working as an effective team, consider how your teamwork can contribute to the transformation of relationships, time, space, and technology.

You may be a leader, an educator, a learner of any age, eager to ignite transformation in the setting of your school, learning ecosystem, institution, district, or other place of work. In any case, if you don't know where to start, or feel you have no power to drive transformation in a whole organization, start by transforming YOURSELF, and you will see how your environment changes.

Small actions can drive BIG CHANGES.

Once you have that in mind, gather your team and think of the shared vision that will guide you in the transformational journey. Wherever you want to start, start with those first milestones that your school or organization can achieve easily so that a positive energy is perceived and sensed in the community, and everyone feels that they want more… Thus, the entire community can embrace the changes which end up driving transformations from the heart.

> *I believe we can create a better world, a better tomorrow, if we work together. Don't you?*
> —Akiroq Brost, Writer & Speaker (Global)

The world is facing significant environmental, social, and economic challenges. Our time is short for addressing those challenges. We can embrace the wisdom of the many voices in this book, including yours, and create a positive future, one team at a time. Form a team, transform your organizational structure, and have some fun along the way! Go teamED!

T ogether
let's **E** mbrace
A wareness on active
tea **M** s
which **E** nable the creation of a
D ifferent world

Your Turn: *Now it's time to write your teamED story.*

Acknowledgments

Our Team is thankful for the conversations and contributions of the many people on six continents who shared their insights into teamwork including Ela Ben-Ur, Suzie Boss, Darlene Cadman, John Franklin Castro Arévalo, Katie Cunningham, Ward Cunningham, Eduard García i Jareño, Alba Gascón Costa, Antonio González Grez Grezan, Clara Patricia Guzmán Silva, Lisa Kerscher, Jennifer Klein, Bob Lenz, Thompson Morrison, Ramon Nogales Romero, Samson Nyikuri Nyongesa, Derek Peterson, Milton Javier Pirazán Rodríguez, Rose Poka, Amaris Salazar, Hana Siddiquee, Kavita Tanna, Anna Tejedor Grifol, Alba Valadez, Louise Whitaker, Daniel Wilson, & Willy Wijnands.

Mar is grateful for the opportunity of co-writing this enlightening book in a collaborative way together with Erin, Nick, and the design flavor of Tegan. Thanks, first, for Nick's invitation to co-write this book with a fully teamed flavor throughout all these years of co-creation; and thanks to Gabriel Diago for inviting me to participate in REC: the Revolution in Education Congress in 2019, where I met Nick. This is where this writing story truly began for me.

Also, I'd like to thank my family, especially my parents for their support in what seemed to be a never-ending story in their eyes. Thanks so much to all the groups and teams I have been a member of in my studies, hobbies and professional career. Thanks to my participation and involvement, thanks to successes, challenges and failures within them, I have been able to gather meaningful insights to learn what worked, and what didn't, and to add to my experience and expertise. Thanks to the Foreign Languages Departments teams and the pedagogical teams in Maristes Champagnat for letting me grow amongst many challenges. And thanks to the MXI team (Xavier Alacid, Pep Buetas, Àlex De la Fuente, Estrella Fustel, Maite Lacasta, Joan Pifarré, Pep Tort, and Miquel Àngel Comas), which allowed me to expand my potential dreaming high in the innovation transformational journey. Thanks to my Toastmasters clubs (Toastmasters 22@Barcelona, Toastmasters Bogotá English Club, and Digital Communicators and One Country One World), which helped me grow as a valuable member of a team within the different leadership teams I was involved in.

Finally, I'd love to thank my current LearnGuides Team at *Learnlife*, for all the opportunities to keep growing as a team member in my lifelong, life-deep and life-wide learning journey. Thanks to Georgi Panayotov, Joan Urgell Farran, Oriol Codina, Caroline Fournier, Maria Galanopoulos, Stephen Harris, Jon Holland, Leticia Lipp, Blair MacLaren, Christopher Pommerening, Olga Prodan, and Emma Buckle. They all are letting me grow within a team of teams.

Erin is grateful for the opportunity to collaborate on this work with such amazing teammates - Nick and Mar. A special thanks to Nick for inviting me into this team and introducing me to Mar and countless partners who have broadened my perspective and impacted my work in their own beautiful and unique ways. For that, I am forever grateful.

This book would not have been possible without the unwavering love and support of my parents, family, and loved ones. Your support has been the cornerstone to who I am and the foundation upon which this work was built. You have been there for me in every way, supporting me to be the best version of myself - whatever that might be. You have provided me guidance and support in acquiring my teaming and collaboration skills and mindsets on the most important team of all, my family.

I am forever appreciative of every team that I have been a member of. With every team, I have been able to practice my teaming and collaborative skills in a variety of ways, only strengthening my belief in the power of teaming and advocacy for it to be common practice. I would especially like to thank my wonderful colleagues at the University of Montana who support my growth and learning in a multitude of different ways.

The Educational Leadership Department has teamed with me throughout my education to prepare me for developing teachers into the professionals the world needs.

The Teaching and Learning Department has provided me with countless opportunities to collaborate with colleagues, community partners, and teacher candidates. Teaming with aspiring educators to support their development into resilient practitioners ready to persist and thrive in our profession. Passing onto them the insights and wisdom that can empower them to become an educator today, for tomorrow.

The Office for Student Success and TRiO for providing me with opportunities to team together with resources across campus to support our students who are experiencing major transition periods. I have gained invaluable insight from working with our first year students and students who are preparing to graduate. Shifting my perspective as a teacher educator to a guide teaming with them to enhance their individual journey through higher education.

The countless students and partners from K-12 and higher education who have pushed me to think big, be curious, engage with an open-mind, be innovative, and not only embrace our diversity but use it to strengthen the communities we belong to and empower each individual in the process.

I am proud to say that the city of Missoula, the state of Montana, and the University of Montana truly has shaped the professional and individual I am today. I am grateful for that and even more passionate about engaging in my work to give back to the community that has shaped and inspired me.

Every teaming opportunity has allowed me to learn, grow, and make impacts farther reaching than ever imagined. It has empowered me in my journey and continues to motivate and inspire me and my work.

Nick is grateful for the sustained energy of co-authors Mar and Erin and the creative insights of Tegan. It has been a remarkable journey with many creative moments, challenges, and growth opportunities along the way. Kavita Tanna committed many hours to carefully reading and editing teamED and has supported me as a life partner in ways beyond measure. Nathan, Sam, and Theo taught me how to be the best cross-generation teammate I could be. Rose Poka, Samson Nyikuri, Anita Jerotich, Beatrice Kamuhu, Jimmie Chengo & Babusi Nygenya demonstrate the resilience and persistence of teams.

Keith Debus, Tom Javins, Geoff Poole, Jack Rowan, Tim Visscher, and Peter Walker-Keleher have nurtured and sustained a safe and supportive gathering of Quaker men. Dean Bennetts taught me about leading diverse teams in education. Fran Locker and Gabriel Diago have been valued teammates multiple times including Revolution in Education Congress, Project Pangea, 24 Hours of PBL+, and much more.

Karen Kelly led many collaborative teams that helped to develop teamED practices. Ideas about teams first emerged while studying and teaching at the University of Cincinnati and Montana State University with Dennis Mann, Bill Widdowson, John Hancock, James Kalsbeek, Shilpa Mehta, and Magdelena Garmaz. Bill Auperlee, RJ Coleman, Jeff Bernstein, Vince DonVito, Mark Ramont, Jill Charles, Patty Hunter, Jim Fyfe, and Ray DeMattis were a part of many vibrant and creative teams from the Dorset Theatre Festival. Grant Taylor continues to be an inspiration for agile teams in the world of comedy, television, and film. Cliff Chisholm, Laura Fedro, Kristin Harding, Rob Pertzborn, and Tad Tsukamoto were an inspiring team from Prugh & Lenon.

My parents Peter & Linda Salmon, in-laws Ghanshyam & Madhu Tanna, my aunts and uncles Joanne & David Weiss and Barbara & Jon Beckwith have each created long-term partnerships we continue to learn from. Tom Salmon, David Sanborn, Tim Sanborn, and David Roth have been teammates in our lifetime together from our adventures in childhood and again as adults.

Tegan is grateful to have been given the opportunity to join Nick, Erin and Mar in the final year of their teamED journey. It's been such a phenomenal time getting a chance to create visual continuity for the stories and teachings they composed in this book. To get the chance to make an impact with my work, to be impacted by those who contributed outside of the authors, and to get to learn from a multitude of minds is both humbling and gratifying.

I would like to thank those who got me here, who encouraged me on my path to becoming a designer and someone who strives for greatness. To my professors at Montana State University, namely Jeffery Conger and Meta Newhouse, thank you for your grace and confidence through the years. Your impact will forever be cherished by me and many others. To my family, especially my parents, Todd and Beth Schaper, thank you for pushing me to be my best because that's the only way to achieve. Thank you for being an excellent example of passionate creativity and sacrifice. I am here because of your support and reassurance.

It has been an overwhelming honor to work with the three minds that made this book a possibility. Thank you, Nick Salmon, for reaching out to me to be a part of this amazing moment in time for the freedom of creativity and for sharing your mind. Thank you, Mar Cano, and your sheer passion for this project, it was both contagious and inspiring. Thank you, Erin O'Reilly, for the encouragement and input on each design how it would impact the project, and its impact on others. All of these people have led to this moment and for that I am thankful.

Our Team

Mar Cano is a dynamic educational professional committed to fostering social transformation through innovative learning practices. With a deep passion for lifelong, life-deep and life-wide learning, she has dedicated more than her 20-year career to advancing education on a glocal scale.

Mar's academic background includes two master's degrees—one in Educational Research and Change, and another one in Representation and Construction of Cultural Identities – complementing her two degrees in Teaching English as a foreign language (EFL) and in English Philology.

Her expertise spans teaching EFL/ESL across all educational levels from preschool to university, and she has also served as a CLIL teacher, university lecturer, pedagogical coordinator, innovation co-leader, and collaborator with NGOs and organizations on projects related to sustainable development and global competencies, early-school dropout, school segregation, and digital equity, among others.

Mar is recognized as an "eduknowmad," engaging in diverse educational roles such as trainer of trainers, facilitator, coordinator, mentor, and speaker. Her work in pedagogical innovation, active methodologies, and alternative paradigms to foster 360 learning has taken her to educational ecosystems worldwide. In recent years, she has focused on teacher training, team leadership and facilitation, and educational and learning innovation both in Catalonia and around the world.

 https://www.linkedin.com/in/marcanoeducation

Erin O'Reilly is a doctoral candidate and adjunct professor in Teaching and Learning at the University of Montana focused on innovative teacher preparation for the world we live in and the world we want to create. Erin is a professionally licensed educator and administrator in Montana. Her academic background includes a Bachelor of Arts in Political Science and History, Master's in Educational Leadership, and doctoral work in Teaching and Learning.

Her expertise as an educational professional has been cultivated through K-12 and higher education teaching experience and participation in state-wide and national organizations. Prior to teaching in higher education, she taught high school social studies. Early in her career, she started as a behavioral intervention specialist. At the University of Montana, she works with teacher candidates advocating for inclusive and collaborative spaces and practices to ensure the success of all learners. She also teaches courses that support students during their transition periods, implementing agile learning and design thinking principles to design their lives while in college and preparing them for what's next after they graduate.

As an educator, she is deeply committed to empowering educators to become agents of change who can make a positive impact on their students and communities. Believing that when students are exposed to diverse cultures, identities, and viewpoints, they develop greater openness, empathy, and critical thinking skills. She collaborates with educators to teach in ways that promote multiculturalism, diversity, and inclusion in their classrooms, curricula, and practices. Looking to innovate and create ways of knowing and doing where all students feel recognized, uplifted, a sense of belonging, and experience success.

https://www.linkedin.com/in/mserinoreilly

Nick Salmon of the Collaborative Learning Network is a ninth-generation educator focused on educational visioning, professional learning experiences for teachers, and design support for future-flexible learning environments.

Recent experiences include Revolution in Education Congress (co-founder), Montana Conference of Educational Leadership, Association For Learning Environments, SXSWEDU, Ohio School Facilities Commission, University of Montana, Montana State University, Harvard University Learning Environments For Tomorrow Institute, Australia Independent Schools Tomorrows Environments for Learning.

His global practice covers 42 US States, 22 time zones, and 35 countries on 6 continents (anxiously awaiting the day penguins in Antarctica begin to advocate for a transformative network of K-12 schools). He is the world's first and only self-certified furniture whisperer, capable of coaxing the best possible performance from the unruliest furnishings.

Nick is the co-founder of a network of collectively flourishing USTAWI Global Learning Communities where relationships, learning, and communities come alive.

https://www.linkedin.com/in/nick-salmon-64619010/

Photo credit: Joann McPike

Tegan Schaper is a graphic designer and illustrator with a BFA from Montana State University, based in Bozeman, Montana. As a budding designer, Tegan's interest in Graphic Design started with a passion for creating and its impact on the world. Drawing and painting are two aspects of her life that were a catalyst for her pursuit of a profession in design. She is passionate about creating an environment that cultivates appreciation and admiration for design and the power it holds.

https://www.linkedin.com/in/tegan-schaper-a6689924a/

References

A quote by Ifeanyi Enoch Onuoha. (n.d.). https://www.goodreads.com/quotes/658233-teamwork-is-the-secret-that-make-common-people-achieve-uncommon.

Agile Manifesto. (2001). https://agilemanifesto.org/.

Allen, S. (2018, May). *The science of gratitude*. Greater Good Science Center, John Templeton Foundation. https://ggsc.berkeley.edu/images/uploads/GGSC-JTF_White_Paper-Gratitude-FINAL.pdf.

Ashoka. (2016, March 29). *How fluid teams create good business*. Medium. https://medium.com/change-maker/how-fluid-teams-create-good-business-c84eeac3976b.

Avdiaj, B. (2017). *Small team effectiveness on decision-making*. [Thesis, University of Prishtina]. http://dx.doi.org/10.13140/RG.2.2.15265.92006

Baker, W., Costa, A., & Shalit, S. (1997). The norms of collaboration: Attaining communicative competence. In A. Costa & R. Liebmann (Eds.), *The process-centered school: Sustaining a renaissance community*. Corwin.

Barth, R. S., & Sizer, T. R. (1991). *Improving schools from within: Teachers, parents, and principals can make the difference*. Wiley.

Berger, R., Vilen, A., & Woodfin, L. (2020). *We are crew: A teamwork approach to school culture*. EL Education.

Blankstein, A. M., & Noguera, P. (2012). *Excellence through equity: Five principles of courageous leadership to guide achievement for every student*. ASCD.

Boroditsky. L. (2017, November). *How language shapes the way we think*. TEDWomen 2017. https://www.ted.com/dubbing/lera_boroditsky_how_language_shapes_the_way_we_think?subtitle=en&audio=pt-br&language=en&utm_campaign=tedspread&utm_medium=referral&utm_source=tedcomshare.

Boss, S. & Larmer, J. (2018). *Project based teaching: How to create rigorous and engaging learning experiences*. ASCD.

Briskin, A., Erickson, S., Callanan, T., & Ott, J. (2009). The power of collective wisdom: And the trap of collective folly. Berrett-Koehler Publishers.

Brost, A. (2023, May 24). *The power of mindfulness: Cultivating awareness and presence in the present moment*. Being Magazine. https://www.wellbeing.com.au/being/author/akiroq-brost/

Brown, B. (2010, June). *The power of vulnerability*. TEDxHouston. https://www.ted.com/talks/brene_brown_the_power_of_vulnerability.

Buchanan, A. (2020). *Benefit mindset schools guide*. Cohere. https://benefitmindset.com/wp-content/uploads/2020/08/BM-Schools-Guide-Aug-2020.pdf.

CAPS International Institute. (2007 - 2021). One World 365. http://www.oneworld365.org/company/caps-international-institute-sl.

Cassel, S. (2019, October 8). *How to choose a co-teaching model knowing the pros and cons of the six models of co-teaching can help teachers determine which one is best for a given lesson*. Edutopia. https://www.edutopia.org/article/how-choose-co-teaching-model.

Center for Applied Special Technology (CAST). (2024). *Universal design for learning framework.* https://www.cast.org/impact/universal-design-for-learning-udl.

Centre for Teaching and Learning. (n.d.). Teamwork and group work. Western University. https://teaching.uwo.ca/teaching/engaging/setting-up-teamwork.html#formation.

The Change Initiative. (n.d.). *The good project research: Impact of design for change 2009 2012.* https://www.dfcworld.com/file2015/research_1.pdf.

Cheng Jie Lee, I., Wong, P., Pei Lin Goh, S. & Cook, S. (2022, April 26). A synchronous hybrid team-based learning class: Why and how to do it? *Medical Science Educator, 32*, 697–702. https://doi.org/10.1007/s40670-022-01538-5.

Chicago Public Schools. (2017). *Restorative practices: Guide and toolkit*. Office of Social & Emotional Learning in collaboration with the Embrace Restorative Justice in Schools Collaborative. https://drive.google.com/file/d/0B18g5ywbF84_bk1nWU96OFdadE0/view.

Ciuta, S. (2023). *The transformative power of daily actions: How your choices shape your character: Day by day what you do is who you become.*

Cline, F. & Fay, J. (2006). *Parenting with love and logic: Teaching children responsibility*. NavPress. Retrieved from https://pdfhive.com/parenting-with-love-and-logic-teaching-children-responsibility/.

Cook, L. & Friend, M. (1993). Educational Leadership for Teacher Collaboration. In Billingsley, B. S., et al. (Eds.) *Program Leadership for Serving Students with Disabilities*. Virginia Polytechnic Institute and State University. https://files.eric.ed.gov/fulltext/ED372540.pdf.

Cook, L. & Friend, M. (2016). *Interactions: Collaboration skills for school professionals*. Pearson.

Costa, A. L. & Kallick, B. (2021). The institute for habits of mind. https://www.habitsofmindinstitute.org/what-are-habits-of-mind/.

Covey, S. (2004). The 7 habits of highly effective people: Powerful lessons in personal change. Free Press.

Creating a better world with character strength. (n.d.). Tilt365. https://www.tilt365.com/about.

CREducation Project. (2007-2024). *'I-messages practice'.* https://creducation.net/activity/i-messages-practice/.

De Bono, E. (1992). *Six thinking hats: Run better meetings, make faster decisions.* Penguin Random House.

Delizonna, L. (2017, August 24). *High-performing teams need psychological safety. Here's how to create it.* Harvard Business Review. https://hbr.org/2017/08/high-performing-teams-need-psychological-safety-hereshow-to-create-it.

Design For Change. (2016). Guide to facilitate projects.

Dewey, J. (1933). *How we think: A restatement of the relation of reflective thinking to the educative process.* D. C. Heath.

Doyle, T. (2023). *Learner-centered teaching: Putting the research on learning into practice.* Taylor & Francis.

Duhill, C. (2016, 25 February). *What Google learned from Its quest to build the perfect team.* The New York Times. https://scholar.harvard.edu/people_analytics/publications/what-google-learned-itsquest-build-perfect-team.

Dumont, H., Istance, D. & Benavides, F. (2010). *The nature of learning: Using research to inspire practice.* OECD Publications.

Duncan-Andrade, J. (2011, September 28). *Growing roses in concrete.* TEDx Golden Gate ED. https://youtu.be/2CwS60ykM8s

Dweck. C. (2006). *Mindset: The new psychology of success.* Random House Publishing Group.

Dweck, C. (2014, December 17). *The power of believing that you can improve* [Video]. YouTube. https://www.youtube.com/watch?v=_X0mgOOSpLU.

EasyRetro. (n.d.). *What went well retrospective - Improve with this easy template.* https://easyretro.io/templates/went-well-to-improve-actionitems/?utm_source=mailchimp&utm_medium=newsletter&utm_campaign=email.

Edmondson, A. (1999). Psychological Safety and Learning Behavior in Work Teams. *Administrative Science Quarterly, 44*(2), 49. Retrieved from https://doi.org/10.2307/2666999.

Edmondson, A. C. (2012). *Teaming: How organizations learn, innovate, and compete in the knowledge economy.* Jossey-Bass.

Educational teams. (n.d.). https://eduteams.iiia.csic.es/login.

eduScrum. (2020, January). *The eduScrum guide: "The rules of the game".* https://slabstatic.com/prod/uploads/oui3ndfr/posts/attachments/7FUalX 0xUgljc_Wyfudi0Vq9.pdf.

Edutopia. (2019, June 27). 60-Second Strategy: SLANT Listening. [Video]. Youtube. https://youtu.be/sU9TumF_Cbo.

Elmore, R. F. (2004). *School reform from the inside out: Policy, practice, and performance.* Harvard Education Press.

Erickson, T. J., & Gratton, L. (2007, November). *Eight ways to build collaborative teams.* Harvard Business Review. https://hbr.org/2007/11/eight-ways-to-build-collaborative-teams.

Ferris, S. P. & Godar, S. H. (2006). *Teaching and learning with virtual teams.* Information Science Publishing.

Fishbone Diagram Overview. (n.d.). High Tech High Graduate School of Education. https://hthgse.edu/resources/fishbone-diagram-overview/

The Foundation. (2020). Freedom Writers Foundation . https://www.freedomwritersfoundation.org/about/.

Fredrickson, B. L. (2004a). Gratitude, like other positive emotions, broadens and builds. In R.A. Emmons & M.E. McCullough (Eds.). *The Psychology of Gratitude.* Oxford University Press.

Fredrickson, B. L. (2004b). The broaden–and–build theory of positive emotions. *Philosophical Transactions of the Royal Society B Biological Sciences, 359*(1449). https://doi.org/10.1098/rstb.2004.1512.

Friedrich, C., Teaford, H., Taubenheim, A., Boland, P. & Sick, B. (2019). Escaping the professional silo: An escape room implemented in an interprofessional education curriculum. *Journal of Interprofessional Care, 33*(5), 573-575. https://doi.org/10.1080/13561820.2018.1538941.

Garmston, R. & Wellman, B. (1999). *The adaptive school: A sourcebook for developing collaborative groups.* Christopher-Gordon.

Gold Standard PBL? (n.d.). Buck Institute for Education. https://www.pblworks.org/what-is-pbl/gold-standard-project-design.

Goldman, S. & Kabayadondo, Z. (2016). *Taking design thinking to school: How the technology of design can transform teachers, learners, and classrooms.* Routledge.

Grant, A. M., & Gino, F. (2010). A little thanks goes a long way: Explaining why gratitude expressions motivate prosocial behavior. *Journal of Personality and Social Psychology, 98*(6), 946-955. https://doi.org/10.1037/a0017935.

Gray, D., Brown, S., & Macanufo, J. (2010). Gamestorming: A playbook for innovators, rulebreakers, and changemakers. O'Reilly.

Green Bronx Machine. (2024). *About.* https://greenbronxmachine.org/.

Habits of Mind Institute. (2016). *Self-assessment rubric.* https://www.habitsofmindinstitute.org/wp-content/uploads/2016/11/S8.5-Part4-Habits-of-Mind-self-assessment.pdf.

Habits of Mind Institute. (n.d.). https://www.habitsofmindinstitute.org/wp-content/uploads/2018/10/HabitsofTheMindChartv2.pdf.

Haglund, E. (1998). What's right with education? Erin Gruwell's reconnecting the disconnected. *Education, 119*(2), 3-13.

Hall, T. E. (2021). *40 beautiful Mother Teresa quotes that remind us to care for others and exemplify Christ's love.* https://www.crosswalk.com/faith/spiritual-life/beautiful-mother-teresa-quotes.html.

Hamelink, C.J. (2020). Communication and peace: Celebrating moments of sheer human togetherness. Palgrave Macmillan.

Hattie, J. & Timperley, H. (2007, March). The power of feedback. *Review of Educational Research, 77*(1), 81-112. https://doi.org/10.3102/003465430298487.

Hayes, P. (2011). *Leading and coaching teams to success: The secret life of teams.* Open University Press.

High Tech High Unboxed. (2017, June 5). Ron Berger - Rules for critique. [Video] Youtube. https://youtu.be/cWMH_X4IvOk.

Hussong, A. (2020, November 24). How to practice gratitude? Notice. Think. Feel. Do. The University of North Carolina at Chapel Hill. https://www.unc.edu/discover/how-to-practice-gratitude-notice-think-feel-do/.

IDEO LLC. (2012). *Design thinking for educators. Toolkit.* https://f.hubspotusercontent30.net/hubfs/6474038/Design%20for%20Learning/IDEO_DTEdu_v2_toolkit+workbook.pdf.

The Importance of Celebrating Milestones. (n.d.). Maryville University. https://online.maryville.edu/blog/importance-of-celebrating-milestones/.

Kagan, S. (1985). Dimensions of cooperative classroom structures. In Slavin, R., Sharan, S., Kagan, R. Lazarowitz, H., Webb, C., & Schmuck, R. (eds.), *Learning to cooperate, cooperating to learn.* Plenum Press.

Kirkman, B., Stoverink, A. C., Mistry, S., & Rosen, B. (2019, July 19). *The 4 things resilient teams do.* Harvard Business Review. Retrieved from https://hbr.org/2019/07/the-4-things-resilient-teams-do.

Klein, J. D. & Ciotti, K. (2022). *The landscape model of learning. Designing student-centered experiences for cognitive and cultural inclusion.* Solution Tree Press.

Kohn, A. (2011, March 6). *The (alternative) schools our kids deserve.* MAAP Conference. https://youtu.be/ephQ8Y8Srkw 238.

Kolb, D. A. (1984). *Experiential learning: Experience as a source of learning and development.* Prentice-Hall.

LaGravenese, R. (2007). *Freedom Writers.* [Film]. MTV Films. Retrieved from https://www.imdb.com/video/vi3634888985?playlistId=tt0463998.

Laloux, F. (2014). *Reinventing organizations: A guide to creating organizations inspired by the next stage of human consciousness.* Nelson Parker.

Larmer, J. & Mergendoller, J.R. (2010). The main course, not Dessert: How are students reaching 21st century goals? With 21st century project based learning. Buck Institute for Education.

Launay, J., & Pearce, E. (2020). Singing as an evolved behavior for social bonding: The ice-breaker effect, beta-endorphins, and groups of more than 150 people. In R. Heydon, D. Fancourt & A.J. Cohen. (Eds.), *The Routledge Companion to Interdisciplinary Studies in Singing, Volume III: Wellbeing.* Routledge. https://doi.org/10.4324/9781315162546.

Lee, D. (2018). *Design thinking in the classroom: Easy-to-use teaching tools to foster creativity, encourage innovation and unleash potential in every student.* Ulysses Press.

Lemov, D. (2010). Teach like a champion: 49 techniques that put students on the path to college. Jossey-Bass.

Lencioni, P. (2002). *Overcoming the five dysfunctions of a team: A field guide for leaders, managers, and facilitators.* Wiley.

Lencioni, P. (2010). *Getting naked: A business fable about shedding the three fears that sabotage client loyalty.* Jossey Bass.

Leonard, K., & Yorton, T. (2015). *Yes, and: How improvisation reverses "no, but" thinking and improves creativity and collaboration--Lessons from the second city.* HarperCollins.

Lobman, C. (2005, July). Yes and": The uses of improvisation for early childhood professional development. *Journal of Early Childhood Teacher Education, 26*(3), 306-307. Vol. 26 (3). https:/doi.org/10.1080/10901020500371353.

Manson-Smith, L., Baltzley, D. R., Ackermann, B., & Vaughn, A. (2021, July 21). The hybrid meeting challenge. https://www.kornferry.com/insights/this-week-in-leadership/the-hybrid-meeting-challenge1.

McChrystal, S., Collins, T., Silverman, D., & Fussell, C. (2015). *Team of teams: New rules of engagement for a complex world.* Portfolio/Penguin.

Nagoski, E., & Nagoski, Amelia. (2019). *Burnout: The secret to unlocking the stress cycle.* Ballantine Books.

NPR. (2023, January 16). *Read Martin Luther King Jr.'s "I Have a Dream" speech in its entirety.* https://www.npr.org/2010/01/18/122701268/i-have-a-dream-speech-in-its-entirety.

OECD. (2016). *Education at a glance 2016: OECD indicators.* OECD Publishing. https://doi.org/10.1787/eag-2016-en.

Other World Escapes. (2021, February). 10 reasons an escape room is the best team building activity: Make great teams. Make great memories. Retrieved from https://www.otherworldescapes.com/blog-post/best-team-building-activity/.

Oviawe, J. (2016). How to rediscover the ubuntu paradigm in education. *International Review of Education, 62*, 1–10. https://doi.org/10.1007/s11159-016-9545-x.

Pan, R., Lo, H. & Neustaedter, C. (2017, June). *Collaboration, awareness, and communication in real-life escape rooms.* School of Interactive Arts and Technology. Simon Fraser University. https://www.researchgate.net/profile/Rui_Pan13/publication/317420614_Collaborati on_Awareness_and_Communication_in_RealLife_Escape_Rooms/links/59a636b2a6fdcc61fcf991ee/Collaboration-Awarenessand-Communication-in-Real-Life-Escape-Rooms.pdf.

PBL Works. (n.d.). *What is PBL?* Buck Institute for Education. https://www.pblworks.org/what-is-pbl.

PBL Works. (2020). *Collaboration rubrics.* Buck Institute for Education. https://my.pblworks.org/node/11282.

Perkins-Gough, D. & Duckworth, A. (2013, January). The significance of grit. *Educational leadership: Journal of the Department of Supervision and Curriculum Development,* 71(1),14-20. https://www.researchgate.net/publication/272078893_The_significance_of_grit.

Perkins, D. & Swartz, R. (1991). The nine basics for teaching thinking. In A. Costa, J. Bellanca, and R. Fogarty (Eds.), If *Minds matter: A foreword to the future.* (pp. 53-70). Skylight Publishing.

Pixelstorm. (2022, December 13). *Famous quotes and stories.* International Churchill Society. https://winstonchurchill.org/resources/quotes/famous-quotations-and-stories/.

Powell, A., Piccoli, G. & Ives, B. (2004). Virtual teams: a review of current literature and directions for future research. *The DATA BASE for Advances in Information Systems - Winter 35(1).*

Project implicit. (2011). *Ethical considerations.* https://implicit.harvard.edu/implicit/ethics.html.

Project Zero. (2015). *Think Pair Share.* Project Zero: Harvard Graduate School of Education. https://pz.harvard.edu/resources/think-pair-share.

Project Zero. (2022). *Thinking routines toolbox.* Harvard Graduate School of Education. https://pz.harvard.edu/thinking-routines.

Quoteresearch. (2019, November 6). *The best way to lift one's self up is to help some one else.* Quote Investigator®. https://quoteinvestigator.com/2019/11/06/lift/

Ramirez, A. (2013, April 2). *Passion-based learning.* Edutopia. https://www.edutopia.org/blog/passion-based-learning-ainissa-ramirez.

Ray, A. (2017). *Mindfulness: Living in the moment, living in the breath.* Inner Light Publishers.

Ritchhart, R. (2015). *Creating cultures of thinking: The 8 forces we must master to truly transform our schools.* Wiley.

Ritchhart, R., Church, M. & Morrison, K. (2011). *Making thinking visible. How to promote engagement, understanding, and independence for all learners.* Jossey-Bass.

Robinson, K. (2010, October 14). Changing Education Paradigm. [Video file]. Retrieved from http://www.thersa.org

Rock, D., Halvorson, H. G. & Grey, J. (2016). *Diverse team.* https://hbr.org/2016/09/diverse-teams-feel-less-comfortable-and-thats-why-theyperform-better.

Rose-Duckworth, R., & Ramer, K. (2008). *Fostering learner independence: An essential guide for K-6 educators*. Corwin Press.

Rothman, J., & Kilby, M. (2019). *From chaos to successful distributed agile teams: collaborate to deliver*. Practical Ink.

Rowell, L. (2023, July 21). *Promoting gratitude in your classroom*. Edutopia. https://www.edutopia.org/article/teaching-ways-express-gratitude.

Ruiz, D. M. (2018). *The four agreements: A practical guide to personal freedom*. Amber-Allen Publishing.

Ruiz, M., & Mills, J. (1997). *The four agreements: A practical guide to personal freedom*. Amber-Allen Publishing.

Sameer, S. J. (2022). *Renowned Japanese poet – Ryunosuke Satoro beautifully equates life and the ocean in his following*. Medium. https://medium.com/@sameer.nilatkar/renowned-japanese-poet-ryunosuke-satorobeautifully-equates-life-and-the-ocean-in-his-following-741632732719.

Savery, J. R. (2006). Overview of problem-based Learning: Definitions and distinctions. *Interdisciplinary Journal of Problem-Based Learning, 1*(1). https://doi.org/10.7771/1541-5015.1002.

Schafer, L. (2018, July 23). *What makes a good school culture?* https://www.gse.harvard.edu/ideas/usable-knowledge/18/07/what-makes-good-school-culture?utm_campaign=Alliance&utm_medium=email&_hsmi=128445999&_hsenc=%20p2ANqtz-8OZ5jWJ2j9jbAn8x2dzO_t5sGjY7s7Tk-LxFn8-GCgAxgPmfi94HopPnQLUR-JiVsuC7GvdM2u40iWOViNAECjEXmswA&utm_content=128445999&utm_source=hs_email.

Schön, D. A. (1983). *The reflective practitioner: How professionals think in action*. Basic Books.

Schwaber, K. & Sutherland, J. (2020, November). *The scrum guide: The definitive guide to scrum: The rules of the game*. https://scrumguides.org/docs/scrumguide/v2020/2020-Scrum-Guide-US.pdf.

Sidky, A. (n.d.). *Agile Mindset*. Ahmed Sidky: Educating for agile mindsets. https://www.ahmedsidky.com/agile-mindset.

Sinek, S. (2014). *Leaders eat last: Why some teams pull together and others don't*. Penguin.

Sinek, S., Mead, D. & Docker, P. (2017). *Find your why: A practical guide for discovering purpose for you and your team*. Portfolio/Penguin.

Swartz, R. Costa, A., Beyer, B, Reagan, R. & Kallick, B. (2008). *Thinking-based learning: Promoting quality student achievement in the 21st century.* Teachers College Press.

Swartz, R. J., & Parks, S. (1994). *Infusing critical and creative thinking into content instruction: A lesson design handbook for the elementary grades.* Critical Thinking Press & Software.

Swartz, R. J., & Perkins, D. N. (1990). *Teaching thinking: Issues and approaches.* Midwest Publications.

Thomas, K. W., & Kilmann, R. H. (2002). *Thomas-Kilmann conflict mode instrument.* CPP, Incorporated.

Thóren, P.M. (2019). *The gardener metaphor for agile leadership.* https://www.linkedin.com/pulse/gardener-metaphor-leadership-pia-maria-thor%C3%A9n/.

Treehouse Innovation. (n.d.). Design thinking at Riverside School. https://treehouseinnovation.com/education-spotlight-design-thinking-at-riverside-school/.

Tzu, L. (1996). *Tao Te Ching* (A. Waley, Trans.). Wordsworth Editions.

UNESCO. (2016). *Education 2030: Incheon declaration and framework for action for the implementation of sustainable development goal 4: Ensure inclusive and equitable quality education and promote lifelong learning opportunities for all.* https://unesdoc.unesco.org/ark:/48223/pf0000245656

The Why of eduScrum. (n.d.). https://eduscrum.org/the-why-of-eduscrum/.

Wikipedia contributors. (2024, August 27). *Maslow's hierarchy of needs.* Wikipedia. https://en.wikipedia.org/wiki/Maslow%27s_hierarchy_of_needs#/media/File:Dynamic_hierarchy_of_needs_-_Maslow.svg.

Wilck, J., & Lynch, P. C. (2018, June). *Diverse teams build better forecasts.* Paper presented at 2018 ASEE Annual Conference & Exposition, Salt Lake City, Utah. 10.18260/1-2–30339.

Wild, M. D., Mayeaux, A. S., & Edmonds, K. (2008). *Teamwork: Setting the standard for collaborative teaching, grades 5-9.* Stenhouse Publishers.

Zak, P. (2018). The neuroscience of high-trust organizations. *American Psychological Association. Consulting Psychology Journal: Practice and Research, 70*(1), 45-58. http://dx.doi.org/10.1037/cpb0000076.

Zenger, J., & Folkman, J. (2019, February 05). *The 3 elements of trust.* Harvard Business Review. https://hbr.org/2019/02/the-3-elements-oftrust.

Additional Resources

Chapter 1 Getting Started

MindsetWorks. (n.d.). *How can mindsets be changed?*
https://www.mindsetworks.com/science/Changing-Mindsets

Team Alignment Company. (2024). *Tools that transform.*
https://www.teamalignment.co/downloads

Chapter 2 Team Formation

Senge, P. (n.d.). *The power of collective wisdom.*
https://www.thepowerofcollectivewisdom.com/pdfs/foreword.pdf

Chapter 3 Team Composition

Dukewits, P. & Gowin, L. (1996). Creating successful collaborative teams. *Journal of Staff Development, 17*(4), 12-16. https://eric.ed.gov/?id=EJ535074

Edcamp Community. (n.d.). Digital Promise. https://digitalpromise.org/edcamp/

EL Education. (n.d.). https://eleducation.org/resources/crew-culture/

Marzano, R. J., Heflebower, T., Hoegh, J. K., Warrick, P., & Grift, G. ((2016). *Collaborative teams that transform schools*: *The next step in PLCs.* Marzano Research.

Mastrogiacomo, S., Osterwalder, A., Smith, A., & Papadakos, T. (2021). *High-impact tools for teams: 5 tools to align team members, build trust, and get results fast.* Wiley.

Solis, M., Vaughn, S., Swanson, E., & Mcculley, L. (2012, 10 April). *Collaborative models of instruction: The empirical foundations of inclusion and co-teaching.* Wiley.

University of Silicon Valley. (2017, May 16). Beginner's guide: How hackathons work as educational models. https://usv.edu/blog/beginners-guide-how-hackathons-work-as-educational-models/

Zoras, B. (2015, July 21). Hackathons as a new pedagogy. Edutopia. https://www.edutopia.org/blog/hackathons-as-a-new-pedagogy-brandon-zoras

Chapter 4 Teamwork Strategies

Amabile, T. M. (2020, May 6). *The power of small wins*. Harvard Business Review. https://hbr.org/2011/05/the-power-of-small-wins

Bedore, B. (2004). *101 Improv Games for Children and Adults.* Hunter House.

Ghafoor, A. (2024). Employee empowerment and organizational performance: Unleashing potential in uncertain times. *Review Journal for Management & Social Practices, 2*(1). https://www.rjmsp.com/index.php/Journal/article/view/18/29

Gonzalez, J. (2023, November 23). *It's Time to Give Classroom Jobs Another Try.* Cult of Pedagogy. https://www.cultofpedagogy.com/classroom-jobs/.

Higger, E. (2019, February 7). *Improv for Educators.* Harvard Graduate School of Education. https://www.gse.harvard.edu/news/19/02/improv-educators.

The jigsaw classroom. (n.d.). https://www.jigsaw.org/#google_vignette.

Lincoln, J. (2022, August 4). *17 inspirational quotes to instantly foster teamwork when unity is lost.* Entrepreneur. https://www.entrepreneur.com/leadership/17-teamwork-quotes-to-inspire-your-employees/269941

Mba, C. M. P. (2024, September 16). *What is negativity bias and how can it be overcome?* PositivePsychology.com. https://positivepsychology.com/3-steps-negativity-bias/

Morgan, B. B., Salas, E., & Glickman, A. S. (1994). An analysis of team evolution and maturation. *The Journal of General Psychology, 120*(3), 277–291.

Shim, J. (2021, July 26). *Team-Building activities to help students reconnect in the classroom.* Edutopia. https://www.edutopia.org/article/team-building-activities-help-students-reconnect-classroom

Staff, N. (2023, August 3). *The 5 biggest biases that affect decision-making.* NeuroLeadership Institute. https://neuroleadership.com/your-brain-at-work/seeds-model-biases-affect-decision-making/

Wheelan, S. A., Åkerlund, M., & Jacobsson, C. (2020). *Creating effective teams: A guide for members and leaders.* SAGE Publications.

Wikipedia contributors. (2024, February 20). *Group development.* Wikipedia. https://en.wikipedia.org/wiki/Group_development#Wheelan%27s_integrated_model_of_group_development

Chapter 5 Teams in Action

About DFC USA. (n.d.). Design for Change. https://www.designforchange.us/pages/about-us

Ahmed Sidky. (2014, July 7). *#7: Agile teams versus organizational agility* [Video]. YouTube. https://www.youtube.com/watch?v=pXJVCKHSoik

Apple. (2008). *Challenge based learning: Take action and make a difference.* Apple, Inc.

Barseghian, T. (2011, July 14). *Nine Tenets of Passion-Based Learning.* KQED. https://www.kqed.org/mindshift/13645/nine-tenets-of-passion-based-learning

Cano, M. (2017, May). EFL Challenging Tasks for Late Teens from a Competencial Approach. In *English Is It!* (ELT Training Series), *8,* 89-101. http://diposit.ub.edu/dspace/bitstream/2445/112923/6/VOLUM%208%20%28ELT%20Training%20Series%29.pdf

Collins, A. & Halverson, R. (2009). *Rethinking Education in the Age of Technology.* The Digital Revolution of Schooling in America. Teachers College. https://journals.oslomet.no/index.php/seminar/article/view/2366/2206

Denning, S. (2022, April 14). *Understanding the agile mindset.* Forbes. https://www.forbes.com/sites/stevedenning/2019/08/13/understanding-the-agile-mindset/

Design for Change - Feel, Imagine, Do and Share (FIDS). (n.d.) https://participedia.net/method/4791

The Good Project Research. (n.d.). Design for change. https://www.dfcworld.com/SITE/Research

DIYLab – Do It Yourself in Education: Expanding digital competence to foster student agency and collaborative learning. (n.d.). https://diylab.eu/

Domingo-Coscollola, M., Arrazola-Carballo, J., & Sancho-Gil, J. M. (2016). Do it yourself in education: Leadership for learning across physical and virtual borders. *International Journal of Educational Leadership and Management, 4*(1), 5-29. doi: 10.17583/ijelm.2016.1842

eduScrum in Class. (2018, 24 Oct). https://youtu.be/uRgBBaiUc58?si=5S_CzZvPZBcTCh0e

eduScrum - Inspired by Students, Teachers & Agilists learning together. (n.d.). https://eduscrum.org/

Edutopia. (2015, February 3). *Service Learning: Real-Life applications for learning* [Video]. YouTube. https://www.youtube.com/watch?v=7t30ZMX8uGw

Edutopia. (2017, April 6). *Design Thinking: Prioritizing process skills* [Video]. YouTube. https://www.youtube.com/watch?v=l7-MVYjZYOE

Edutopia. (2018, September 19). *Design Thinking: a problem solving framework* [Video]. YouTube. https://www.youtube.com/watch?v=kfBa2AdjRB4

Edutopia. (2023, July 19). *Creating a culture of caring through Student-Led Service learning* [Video]. YouTube. https://www.youtube.com/watch?v=3_7zJ6Lm5-A

Essential Readings in Problem-based Learning. (2015). United States: Purdue University Press.

Future Learning Design Podcast. (2020, May 10) EduScrum in the classroom - A conversation with Willy Wijnand. https://open.spotify.com/episode/5jPN8UT0LWQrlMmquCvPJs?si=e3jMlhDkQs6Nbsqhhdnt3Q

Guzzetti, B., Elliott, K., & Welsch, D. (2010). *DIY Media in the Classroom.* Teachers College Press

IDEO U. (2021, May 26). *What is Design Thinking?* [Video]. YouTube. https://www.youtube.com/watch?v=QWdgcpAHRlM

Jeavon, B. (2020, November 23). *How to deploy agile in education and create self lead student teams with Willy Wijnands.* EnterpriseExcellence Podcast. https://www.enterpriseexcellenceacademy.com/podcast/episode/4b784da6/13-how-to-deploy-agile-in-education-and-create-self-lead-student-teams-with-willy-wijnands

Krehbiel, T. K., Salzaruloa, P. A., Cosmaha, M. L., Forrena, J., Gannodb, G., Havelka, D., Hulshult, A. R., & Merhout, J. (2017). Agile Manifesto for Teaching and Learning. *The Journal of Effective Teaching, 17*(2), 90-111.

Kafai, Y. & Peppler, K. (2011). Youth, technology, and DIY: developing participatory competencies in creative media production. In V. L. Gadsden, S. Wortham, and R. Lukose (Eds.), *Youth Cultures, Language and Literacy. Review of Research in Education, 34.* https://doi.org/10.3102/0091732X10383211.

Lankshear, C. & Knobel, M. (Eds.). (2010). "DIY Media: A contextual background and some contemporary themes". In *DIY MEDIA: Creating, sharing and learning with new technologies, 44* (pp.1-24). Peter Lang Publishing.

Lara, M., & Lockwood, K. (2016). Hackathons as Community-Based Learning: a Case Study. *TechTrends*, *60*(5), 486–495. https://doi.org/10.1007/s11528-016-0101-0

Learning to Give. (2017, July 6). *Stages of service learning* [Video]. YouTube. https://www.youtube.com/watch?v=kFd-yiAfrmE

Learnlife. (2023, May 18). *Acesco x Learnlife: Hacking the state curriculum with Passion Projects* [Video]. YouTube. https://www.youtube.com/watch?v=z_Ic0cYZiPM

Lee, D. (2018). *Design thinking in the classroom: Easy-to-use teaching tools to foster creativity, encourage innovation and unleash potential in every student.* Ulysses Press.

Magalhães, F. & Valente, X. (2020, 3 Sep). *eduScrum: Contagiando de agilidad a la educación*. K21. https://k21.global/es/blog/eduscrum-contagiando-de-agilidad-a-la-educacion

Munro, D. (2015). Hosting hackathons a tool in retaining students with beneficial side effects. *Journal of Computing Sciences in Colleges*. https://doi.org/10.5555/2752981.2752994

MUSE Virtual. (2021, May 26). *MUSE virtual school - Passion based learning - James Cameron and Suzy Amis Cameron* [Video]. YouTube. https://www.youtube.com/watch?v=N7mA7YL5UGY

National Youth Leadership Council. (2016, November 30). *Project-based learning vs. service-learning* [Video]. YouTube. https://www.youtube.com/watch?v=6avu1dcKlNs

Open Colleges. (2014, February 22). *Agile based learning: What is it and how can it change education?* https://www.opencolleges.edu.au/blogs/articles/agile-based-learning-what-is-it-and-how-can-it-change-education

Peha, S. (2011, June 28). *Agile schools: How technology saves education (just not the way we thought it would)*. InfoQ. https://www.infoq.com/articles/agile-schools-education/

The PBL Institute. https://thepblinstitute.com/

Ramirez, A. (2013, April 2). *Passion-based learning*. Edutopia. https://www.edutopia.org/blog/passion-based-learning-ainissa-ramirez

Schurr, M. (n.d.). *Design thinking for educators* (2nd
    Edition). https://f.hubspotusercontent30.net/hubfs/6474038/Design%20f
    or%20Learning/IDEO_DTEdu_v2_toolkit+workbook.pdf

Scrum at School. (2015, April 13). *The importance of Scrum for education* [Video].
    YouTube. https://www.youtube.com/watch?v=xrk3CU3nW0Y

Scrum Inc. (2020, September 21). *Scrum & eduScrum: Prepare the workforce of
    tomorrow with Dr. Jeff Sutherland and Willy Winjnands* [Video].
    YouTube. https://www.youtube.com/watch?v=iA9bWvnHDrM

Sethi, K. (n.d.). *Kids, take charge* [Video]. TED
    Talks. https://www.ted.com/talks/kiran_sethi_kids_take_charge?language
    =en

Skillen, P. (2019, May 23). *The science of passion based learning*. Powerful Learning
    Practice. https://plpnetwork.com/2013/04/09/memorize-mesmerize/

Remagine Schools. (2019, October 28).*Passion-Based Learning with Derek McCoy
    by Reimagine Schools*. https://podcasters.spotify.com/pod/show/greg-
    goins/episodes/Passion-Based-Learning-with-Derek-McCoy-e8aufu/a-
    autejt

Sprouts. (2016, August 22). *What science knows about learning with passion*
    [Video]. YouTube. https://www.youtube.com/watch?v=JawhTCCbVZM

Staff, T. (2021, November 18). *25 ways to promote passion-based learning in your
    classroom*. TeachThought.
    https://www.teachthought.com/learning/passion-based-learning/

Sutherland, J. (2014). *SCRUM: The art of doing twice the work in half the time*.
    Crown Business.

TEDx Talks. (2013, March 21). *Design thinking -- Maximizing your students' creative
    talent: Co Barry at TEDxDenverTeachers* [Video].
    YouTube. https://www.youtube.com/watch?v=nyt4YvXRRGA

Tishman, S., & Perkins, D. (2022, February 27). *Episode 2: Mighty metacognition*.
    Thinkability. https://thinkability.substack.com/p/episode-2-mighty-
    metacognition?utm_source=url.

Using roles in teams. (n.d.). MyPBLWorks. https://my.pblworks.org/resource/using-
    roles-teams

Why Design Thinking Guide. (n.d.). Design for Change . https://dtg.dfcworld.org/

Wikipedia contributors. (2024, August 27). *Maslow's hierarchy of needs.* https://en.wikipedia.org/wiki/Maslow%27s_hierarchy_of_needs#/media/File:Dynamic_hierarchy_of_needs_-_Maslow.svg

Wolpert-Gawron, H. (2016, November 7). *What the heck is service learning?* Edutopia. https://www.edutopia.org/blog/what-heck-service-learning-heather-wolpert-gawron

Chapter 6 Teams & Transformation

16Personalities. (n.d.). https://www.16personalities.com/

Campus Virtual EduCaixa Challenge 2021. (2021, June 28). EducaixaTV [Youtube]. https://youtu.be/sT6YRPlJ5so?si=-bGwncH9ecYKVQjE.

Ciuta, S. (2023). *Leadership Unleashed: Inspiring excellence.* Independent Publisher.

Dillenbourg, P. (1999). *Collaborative learning: Cognitive and computational approaches.* Emerald Group Publishing Limited.

eduTEAMS. (n.d.). https://eduteams.org/

EduScrum Guides (2.0). (n.d.). Slab. https://art2beagile.slab.com/public/posts/edu-scrum-guides-2-0-fk6r8ill.

Harvard implicit association test. (2011). Harvard University Project implicit. https://implicit.harvard.edu/implicit/takeatest.html.

Jacobs, G. M., Gan, S. L., &Ball, J. (1997). *Learning cooperative learning via cooperative learning: A sourcebook of lesson plans for teacher education on cooperative learning.* Kagan Cooperative Learning.

Johnson, D. W., Johnson, R. T., & Holubec, E. J. (1986). *Circles of learning: Cooperation in the classroom.* Interaction Book Company.

Johnson, D., & Johnson, R. (1987). *Learning together and alone.* Prentice-Hall.

Knutson, J. (2018, January 11). *Setting up effective group work.* Edutopia. *https://www.edutopia.org/article/setting-effective-group-work*

La escuela lo primero. (2022, October 25). La Escuela Lo Primero. https://laescuelaloprimero.cotec.es/.

Lencioni, P. (2002). *The Five Dysfunctions of a Team: A Leadership Fable.*

Meehan, W. F. & Jonker, K. S. (2018, May 30). *Team of teams: An emerging organizational model.* Forbes. https://www.forbes.com/sites/meehanjonker/2018/05/30/team-of-teams-an-emerging-organizational-model/?sh=b7caaf16e790

Mischel, W. (2014). The marshmallow test: Mastering self-Control. Little, Brown Spark.

Participate in the first global online hackathon for children to create solutions to the corona pandemic. (2023, October). Swedish Institute. https://si.se/en/the-first-global-online-hackathon-for-children-to-create-solutions-to-the-corona-pandemic/.

Project READY: reimagining equity & access for diverse youth. (2024). Project READY. https://ready.web.unc.edu/.

Chapter 7 Reflection, Inspiration & Action
Follow up with the team!

Mar Cano Mesa   https://www.linkedin.com/in/marcanoeducation
Erin O'Reilly   https://www.linkedin.com/in/mserinoreilly
Nick Salmon   https://www.linkedin.com/in/nick-salmon-64619010/
Tegan Schaper   https://www.linkedin.com/in/tegan-schaper-a6689924a/

Closing Thoughts

Your Final Turn: How has this book transformed your thinking about teams?